Preaching Through the Year

52 Motivational Messages

Preaching Through the Year

52 Motivational Messages

Dr. David C. Cooper

Pathway
PRESS

Book Editor: Wanda Griffith
Editorial Assistant: Tammy Hatfield
Copy Editors: Esther Metaxas
Jessica Sirbaugh

Library of Congress Catalog Card Number: 2006938767
ISBN: 978-1-59684-255-7
Copyright © 2006 by Pathway Press
Cleveland, Tennessee 37311
All Rights Reserved
Printed in the United States of America

Dedication

This book is dedicated to my only mentor in ministry,

Dr. Paul Walker,

whose pastoral preaching taught me the art of preaching
for the glory of God and the blessing of humanity.

Contents

Foreword

In writing to the Romans the apostle Paul said, "I magnify my ministry [office]" (11:13, *NASB*). Another translation expresses the deep meaning of this verse, "I will take pride in my work" (*CEV*). Someone has said, "The dignity of the ministry (office) of a pastor is determined by the dignity of the appointing power." We are told in Ephesians, "It was he [God] who gave some to be . . . pastors . . . to prepare God's people for works of service, so that the body of Christ may be built up until we all reach unity in the faith and in the knowledge of the Son of God and become mature, attaining to the whole measure of the fullness of Christ" (4:11-13).

Carefully analyze the admonition to pastors in verses 12 and 13: "To prepare God's people for works of service . . . and become mature, attaining to the whole measure of the fullness of Christ." This is a sacred trust; a week-in and week-out holy responsibility. The task takes on many forms, but the central priority is preaching.

John MacArthur said, "Among the varied responsibilities assigned to a pastor, that of preaching stands head and shoulders above the rest in importance. The God-ordained means to save, sanctify, and strengthen His church is preaching." A pastor must determine to be "mighty in the Scriptures" (Acts 18:24, *NASB*) and that he was called to "fully carry out the preaching of the word of God" (Colossians 1:25, *NASB*).

Preaching is a sober and sacred responsibility. The minister speaks for God (see 1 Peter 4:11). This indicates that he must stay close to God through prayer and hearing from God. When I pastored the Metropolitan Church in Birmingham, Alabama, I spent 40 to 50 hours each week in prayer and study. The median time in sermon preparation is one hour of study per minute of preaching time. After pastoring the same church for 23 years, I needed sermon resources from many different sources.

I found that inspiration for sermons came from five different sources: (1) communion with God, (2) current events, (3) crisis situations, (4) conference sessions, and (5) colleagues' sermons. I found both inspiration and insights from the sermons and sermon materials from my colleagues in ministry. The Lord spoke to me through their interpretation and application of Scriptural truths and life situations. *Preaching Through the Year: 52 Motivational Messages*, by David C. Cooper, is an excellent resource in sermon preparation. Dr. Cooper, senior pastor of the Mount Paran Central Church of God in Atlanta, Georgia, is a colleague in ministry. He knows how to relate to fellow pastors, and he knows how to relate to the needs and aspirations of his congregation. He is touched by God to touch His people and to touch other pastors through his resource materials that include books and tapes on prophecy, success, spiritual warfare, Christian service and Bible study.

You will find the sermons in this volume to be faith-based, field-tested and fruit-bearing. They will inspire your personal faith and will trigger thoughts and concepts to personalize the material for your local congregation. The Scriptural interpretations are well grounded, the stories are fresh, and the life applications are relevant—focusing on everyday challenges and opportunities.

As I looked through the book, I found sermons and stories for every occasion, a wealth of material to assist pastors in feeding their flocks. Dr. Cooper is a visionary leader in church growth and in proclaiming the gospel with color, clarity and convictions. The book has blessed and inspired me, and I know it will be a fresh "well" of creative ideas for you in sermon preparation. I am honored to recommend it.

—Raymond F. Culpepper, D.D.
First Assistant General Overseer
Church of God
Cleveland, Tennessee

Introduction

Preaching is risky business. The thought of standing before others and speaking in God's name is sobering. I wonder if God doesn't occasionally lean over heaven's balcony and say in response to some sermons, "Hey, I never said that!" But in spite of our frailties, God has commissioned us to speak "the very words of God" (1 Peter 4:11).

Phillips Brooks was right when he said, "Preaching is truth through personality." And do our personalities ever come through! Preaching is marred by the preacher's emotions, attitudes, sins and struggles. After a while a congregation learns to read the pastor like a book. They monitor his or her facial expressions, body language, appearance, and tone of voice. They know if we're living the overcoming life or the overwhelmed life.

I've experienced moments of sheer spiritual joy while preaching, caught up like the Revelator "in the Spirit on the Lord's Day" (1:10, *NKJV*). And I've been in that lonely place, preaching and thinking to myself, *God, where are You?*

Every minister struggles with the task of preaching—coming up with new material, looking for innovative ways to share the "old, old story of Jesus and His love" with fresh insights and cultural relevance.

I have not written this book for preachers to take the messages and preach them verbatim, but to motivate preachers to understand the structure of a sermon and to stimulate them to wholesome thinking about important Biblical themes. As you read them, I pray that your creativity will kick into gear and that the Holy Spirit will awaken your mind to build on these messages to create your own material. Think of this book like a set of jumper cables to jumpstart your spiritual battery of creativity.

As you go about the task of telling others about God through preaching, remember three important lessons I have learned:

First, don't take yourself too seriously. No one else does. Trust the Holy Spirit to do the work in the hearts of the listeners. John Wesley said, "Prepare the sermon as if there were no Holy Spirit, then preach as if there were no sermon."

Second, God uses imperfect vessels. As Paul observed, "God chose the foolish things of the world to shame the wise" (1 Corinthians 1:27). You don't have to preach perfect sermons to make an impact in people's lives. You just need to exalt Jesus, stick with the Scripture, and be open and honest with your listeners.

Third, and most importantly, be yourself. Allow Christ to shine through the uniqueness of your personality, with all its strengths and weaknesses, as you speak for God. Shakespeare's advice is most apropos for preachers: "To thine own self be true."

The Confidence Quotient

Text: Joshua 1:1-9

Two cows were grazing in a pasture when they saw a milk truck pass. On the side of the truck were the words "Pasteurized, homogenized, standardized, vitamin A added." One cow sighed and said to the other, "Makes you feel sort of inadequate, doesn't it?"

I'm sure that's how Joshua must have felt when God called him to succeed Moses. Moses . . .

- the man of God
- the man who withstood Pharaoh and brought Egypt to its knees
- the man who parted the Red Sea
- the man who brought manna from heaven
- the man who brought water from the rock
- the man who received the Law of God in stone
- the man who spoke with God face-to-face

- the man who saw the glory of God
- the man who led Israel through the wilderness for 40 years.

Moses, however, would not lead Israel into the Promised Land. This would be the responsibility of Joshua, Moses' personal aid and close friend, who had accompanied Moses through the wilderness years.

What Joshua needed was a dose of God-inspired confidence. Confidence is simply a feeling of trust, reliance, faith, and certainty in someone or something. Not self-confidence but Christ-confidence. Joshua's name was really a new name given to him by Moses. His original name was *Hoshea* (Numbers 13:8), meaning "salvation." *Joshua* means "The Lord is salvation," with emphasis on *the Lord.* Joshua was indeed the instrument God used, but the Lord himself was the source of victory.

Notice how often Scripture exhorts us to confident living:

- Proverbs 3:26: "For the Lord will be your confidence and will keep your foot from being snared."

- Jeremiah 17:5, 7: "This is what the Lord says: 'Cursed is the one who trusts in man, who depends on flesh for his strength and whose heart turns away from the Lord. . . . But blessed is the man who trusts in the Lord, whose confidence is in him.'"

- Philippians 1:6: "Being confident of this, that he who began a good work in you will carry it on to completion."

- Hebrews 10:35: "Do not throw away your confidence."

- Hebrews 13:6: "So we say with confidence . . ."

- 1 John 4:17: "We will have confidence on the day of judgment."

THREE PROMISES OF GOD
TO INSPIRE CONFIDENCE

I.   I Will Give You Every Place You Set Your Foot (vv. 3, 4).

A. The Lord spoke to Joshua. Until now the Lord had spoken to Joshua through Moses, but now He spoke directly, personally. Each of us as a priest before God has access to the Father by the Holy Spirit. God speaks to us by His Spirit, giving us confidence. He speaks through Scripture and also in the secret place of our own souls.

B. "I will give you every place where you set your foot, as I promised Moses" (v. 3). Divine promise, plus human responsibility, equals success. God gave the land, but the people had to possess it. Even so, we, by faith, claim the promises of God. We have to "set our foot" on the promise for it to be a reality. God looks for active faith, not passive faith.

C. The warrior spirit. We are too easily discouraged and intimidated in our faith. We, too, develop the "grasshopper syndrome" (see Numbers 13:31-33). We need the spirit of Joshua and Caleb, who were willing to possess the Promised Land (see 14:6-9).

II. **I Will Be With You as I Was With Moses (v. 5).**

A. "No one will be able to stand up against you." Why? Because he was doing the will of God. The promise does not pertain to self-interests but to acting on the will of God. Herein lies our confidence (see Deuteronomy 28:2, 7; Matthew 16:18).

B. "I will be with you as I was with Moses." God was with Moses in . . .

1. *Providential care*: Protected from harm while confronting Pharaoh (see Isaiah 43:1-3).

2. *Limitless sufficiency*: On Mount Sinai he meets God as the great "I Am," meaning, I will be what you need in every situation. He met Jehovah, the promise keeper (Philippians 4:19).

3. *Divine authority*: God transformed his shepherd's rod into a sign of authority. With his shepherd's rod, he

smote the Nile, and it turned to blood; he struck down the false gods of Egypt; he separated the Red Sea (see Luke 10:19).

4. *Miracle power:* Through the power of God, the destroyer of the firstborn smote Egypt, the sea parted, manna came from heaven, water issued forth from the rock, the cloud guided them through the desert, they were victorious in battle (see John 14:12).

5. *Close friendship:* God spoke with Moses face-to-face as a man speaks to his friend (Exodus 33:11).

III. I Will Never Leave You (vv. 5-9).

A. The Biblical concept of the presence of God is more than His omnipresence; it is His active, powerful presence in our lives.

B. The presence of God is a . . .

1. Guiding presence (Exodus 33:14)
2. Protective presence (Psalm 23:4)
3. Joyful presence (16:11)
4. Reassuring presence (Matthew 18:20)
5. Comforting presence (John 14:18).

Illustration

A man once asked me the meaning of Christ praying from the cross, "My God . . . why have you forsaken me?" (Matthew 27:46; Mark 15:34) if God never leaves us. I explained that Christ was experiencing the depth of human loneliness and alienation brought on by becoming our sin. Sin makes us feel estranged from God, fearful that God has abandoned us like cosmic orphans in the universe. That's the feeling: "My God, why have You left me?" But the fact is: "I will never leave you." So we hear the psalmist declare of the Christ, "You will not abandon me to the grave . . . you will fill me with joy in your presence" (16:10, 11).

When Faith Really Counts

Text: Job 2:1-13

He was a righteous man who feared God and shunned evil. He was a family man who had seven sons and three daughters. He was an influential man—regarded as the greatest man in the East. He was a religious man who worshiped God faithfully, offering the burnt offering—an Old Testament offering signifying complete dedication to God.

Job was the envy of the community. He had life just like he wanted it. But suddenly, almost overnight, his fortune changed. A raiding band of mercenaries plundered his possessions and killed his workers. A hurricane struck the house where his 10 children had gathered at his oldest son's house, resulting in their tragic deaths. His body broke out in painful sores from the top of his head to the soles of his feet.

His wife, understandably, fell into depression and bitterness toward God and life. She confronted her husband with a soul-searching question: "Are you still holding on to your integrity?" (v. 9). In other words, "Are you still so naive to believe in God and His goodness?" Then she uttered words which make my soul tremble: "Curse God and die! Give up your faith, Job. Give up on life."

What amazes me about Job is the fact that Job knew when faith really counts. Faith counts in the crucible of life. Faith counts in the face of unanswered questions. Faith counts when we've lost that which is dearest to us.

In a Gallup Poll taken several years ago, people were asked the following question: "If you were to meet God face-to-face and ask Him one question, what would you ask?" The number one response was, "Why is there suffering in the world?" We've been asking the question since Adam and Eve sinned in Eden. The answer is really quite simple: When sin entered the world, death entered. The world is imperfect. In spite of technology, science and developments, the world remains imperfect, and none of us is exempt from the statistical probabilities of life. Jesus said, "These things have I spoken to you, that in Me you may have peace. In the world you will have tribulation; but be of good cheer, I have overcome the world" (John 16:33, *NKJV*).

The question is raised, "Why do the righteous or the innocent suffer?" Job had three close friends who came and debated the issue with him until he was wearied listening to their theological presuppositions. The righteous suffer for the same reason the unrighteous suffer—the world is imperfect, and no one is exempt from suffering.

Why the righteous suffer is not the question we need to be asking. The real question is, What do the righteous do when they suffer? The difference between the righteous and the unrighteous, the believer and the unbeliever, is not in who suffers and who doesn't suffer; the difference exists in how they handle suffering.

Job's experience doesn't teach us why the righteous suffer, it teaches what the righteous do *when* they suffer. What did Job do?

1. He fell to the ground and worshiped (Job 1:20, 21).

2. "In all this, Job did not sin by charging God with wrongdoing" (v. 22).

3. He said, "I know that my Redeemer lives" (19:25).

4. He said, "I have treasured the words of his mouth more than my daily bread" (23:12).

His faith boiled down to one great affirmation: "Though He slay me, yet will I trust Him" (13:15, *NKJV*). Job was not a supersaint. Job hurt deeply. Job was confused, struggling with the question "Why?" But in the midst of his struggle, he held on to his faith. Job knew when faith really counts. Trust means "Don't doubt in the dark what God has shown you in the light."

> *Trusting God.* A very devout Christian who had reached the age of 105 suddenly stopped going to church. Alarmed by his absence after so many years of faithful attendance, the pastor went to see him. He found the man in good health, so the pastor asked him, "How come after all these years we don't see you at the services?" The old fellow looked around, lowered his voice and whispered, "I'll tell you, Pastor: When I got to be 90, I thought God would take me. So then I got to be 95, then 100, then 105. So I figured that God is busy and He must have forgotten about me, and I don't want to remind Him." *(Illustration)*

What can we learn from Job?

I. **Job Trusted the Character of God in Spite of Unanswered Questions.**

    He refused to blame God, or to charge God with wrong-doing (1:21, 22).

    A. The justice of God was on trial. We call this the doctrine of theodicy—the justice of God in light of human suffering. Problem:

        1. How can God's justice be defended in light of suffering?
        2. How can we say that God is good when we see war and oppression in the world?
        3. Or when we walk through a children's cancer ward?
        4. Or when we drive through a ghetto?
        5. Or see people sleeping on the streets?

    B. The conclusions of Job's friends on suffering: Either . . .

        1. God is not Almighty—that is, He doesn't have the power to end suffering.

2. God is not just—or He is evil and good.
3. Man is innocent—he doesn't deserve any of the suffering in our world.
4. The final conclusion of these positions is that a person's suffering is indicative of the measure of his guilt in God's eyes—the essence of karma in Hinduism, which gave rise to the caste system.

C. The conclusion of Job on suffering: There exists an alien presence in the world. Not only are God and man involved in the suffering, but Satan is here. The sin problem brought the curse of the earth. In the midst of a world of evil and, consequently, suffering, God is good and just and merciful. Job meets God during his suffering, but his question "Why?" is never answered.

D. God is good in a world where bad things happen. Romans 8:28 is one of the most misunderstood and misused verses in Scripture. Paul says that "in all things God works for the good of those who love him." This doesn't mean that God causes all things to happen but that God works for our good in spite of what happens.

Illustration

Corrie ten Boom, in her book *Tramp for the Lord*, cites an anonymous poem titled "The Weaver":

My life is but a weaving, between my God and me.
I cannot choose the colors, He worketh steadily.
Ofttimes He weaveth sorrow, and I in foolish pride,
Forget He sees the upper, and I the underside.
Not till the loom is silent, and the shuttles cease to fly,
Will God unroll the canvas and explain the reason why.
The dark threads are as needful in the Weaver's skillful hand,
As the threads of gold and silver in the pattern He has planned.

II. Job Worshiped in Spite of Personal Pain.

A. Can we fully understand his pain? I know that some of you identify well with Job's pain. You have been there. Listen to his lament:

1. "After this, Job opened his mouth and cursed the day of his birth" (3:1).
2. "What I feared has come upon me" (v. 25).
3. "[Oh] that God would be willing to crush me, to let loose his hand and cut me off!" (6:9).
4. "I loathe my very life; therefore I will give free rein to my complaint and speak out in the bitterness of my soul" (10:1).
5. "Man born of woman is of few days and full of trouble" (14:1).
6. "My spirit is broken, my days are cut short, the grave awaits me" (17:1).
7. "I am reduced to dust and ashes" (30:19).
8. "Yet when I hoped for good, evil came; when I looked for light, then came darkness" (v. 26).
9. "The churning inside me never stops; days of suffering confront me" (v. 27).

B. The paradox of worship: In spite of these feelings, he worships God. Worship opens the way for an encounter with God's greatness (chs. 38–41).

During my first pastorate, one of our members asked me to visit a friend dying with Lou Gehrig's disease. I'll never forget that afternoon when I walked into a simple mobile home to pray for this man. She had been bringing him tapes from our worship services, and he wanted to meet me. So I went. As I walked into his bedroom, he greeted me with a big smile. Talking was extremely difficult for him because of the breathing apparatus. He gasped for every breath. Yet, he shared with me the joy that Christ had brought into his life. I prayed for him and bid him goodbye. As I turned to leave, he called to me. "Pastor," he said, "I may give out, but I will never give up."

Illustration

III. Job Regained What He Lost (ch. 42).

God restored to Job what he had lost. Job could have ended in tragedy, bitter toward God, following his wife's advice to curse God and die. Instead, he rose on the wings of faith and became more than a conqueror. Job's strategy was fourfold:

A. Look up: "I know that You can do all things" (v. 2).
B. Look in: "I abhor myself, and repent in dust and ashes" (v. 6, *NKJV*).
C. Look out: He prayed for his friends (see vv. 7-10).
D. Look ahead: God blessed him with "twice as much" (v. 10). Look at the names of his daughters:
   1. *Jemimah* means "dove."
   2. *Keziah* means "cinnamon."
   3. *Keren-Happuch* means "container of antimony," an expensive eye shadow. The names reflect their beauty. They received an inheritance with their brothers. Job was into women's equality. He died at 140 years. He was probably about 70 when tragedy struck his life.

The Way Out of Worry

Text: Matthew 6:25-34

Justice Oliver Wendell Holmes sat one day, distressed. His wife wrote him a note and left it in his study. It read: "You have suffered through many troubles in life—most of which have never happened."

Regardless of who we are, we all deal with the problem of worry. *Worry* can be defined as "an anxious, troubled or fearful state of mind." Someone has said that worry is thinking with our emotions.

Worriers experience the phenomenon of the "racing mind," characterized by an endless stream of anxious thoughts that seem unstoppable. With worry comes increased muscle tension, upset stomach, anxiety and depression, which leads to more serious health problems. Chronic worriers often suffer low self-esteem.

The Greek word means "to be divided or inwardly distracted." The Anglo-Saxon derivative means "to choke or strangle." E.S. Jones said, "Worry is the sand in the machinery of life." On a more humorous note, "worry is today's mouse eating tomorrow's cheese."

Worry is like a rocking chair; it gives you something to do, but gets you nowhere. I like the beatitude that says, "Blessed is the man who is too busy to worry during the day, and too sleepy to worry at night."

The Bible addresses the problem of worry head-on. Worry is no respecter of persons (see Psalm 37:1; Mark 4:18, 19; Luke 21:34; 1 Peter 5:7). The only antidote to worry is the peace that God gives. He will keep us in perfect peace as our minds are fixed on Him (Isaiah 26:3, 4).

We sometimes worry about what people think. Recently, I read: "At age 20, we worry about what others think of us. At 40, we don't care what they think of us. At 60, we discover they haven't been thinking about us at all."

We worry about money. "Why can't you sleep?" the wife asked her husband, who was pacing the floor at 3 a.m. "Honey, I borrowed $1,000 from Sam next door, and I owe it to him by tomorrow," he said, wringing his hands. "I just don't have the money!" His wife jumped out of bed and flung open the window. "Sam," she shouted, "Sam! Sam!" Finally, the groggy neighbor opened the window. "What is it?" he asked. "You know the $1,000 my husband owes you? He doesn't have it." She slammed the window shut. "Now," she told her husband, "you go to sleep and let him worry about the money."

Jesus teaches us how to practice the peace He has given us as a gift (see John 14:27).

I. Observe God's Care in Creation (Matthew 6:25-29).
The doctrine of divine providence is in view. "Look at the birds of the air and the lilies of the field." Deism states that God created the world but has left it to our own devices. Deism is Bette Midler singing, "God is watching us from a distance." But providence means that God is Creator and that He cares for and watches over His creation (see Deuteronomy 33:27; Psalm 91:1; Isaiah 41:10; Matthew 10:29-31; Jude 24).

II. Surrender to God What You Cannot Control (v. 27).
A. Jesus asks a provocative question: "Who of you by worrying can add a single hour to his life?" Recognize the limitations of worry.

God Box. What we need is a "God box." Put your cares and worries in the God box and leave them there. There are people and situations you simply cannot control. Only God can reach them or change the situation. Who or what are you worrying about today that you need to put in the God box?

Illustration

    B. Here are three lessons about worry:

        1. *Worry is an exercise in futility.* Worry won't pay the bills, secure a job promotion, restore a marriage, control your children, heal sickness, or make you happy. Besides, 92 percent of the things we worry about never happen, and the other 8 percent we end up handling.

        2. *Worry is a luxury no one can afford.* Worry is a contributing factor in high blood pressure, arthritis, heart disease and ulcers. One study of 450 people who lived to be 100 years old or older found that these people lived long for the following reasons:

           a. They kept busy.

           b. They used moderation in all things.

           c. They ate lightly and simply.

           d. They got a great deal of fun out of life.

           e. They were early to bed and early up.

           f. They were free from worry and fear, especially fear of death.

           g. They had serene minds and faith in God (Norman Vincent Peale, *The Power of Positive Thinking,* p. 123).

        3. *Worry is contrary to the Christian life of faith.* Worry is a divided mind between faith and fear. Focus your mind purely on the promises of God and overcome your doubts and fears.

III. Focus Your Faith on the Eternal (vv. 32, 33).

    A. *The pagans run after these things.* The material world is important. We all need food, clothing, shelter. We need love, belonging and self-worth. But the pagan lifestyle is consumed with the material.

B. *Seek first the kingdom of God.* Worry is so often focused
    on things that are temporary. We need an eternal perspec-
    tive in a temporal world and remember the things that real-
    ly matter. Eternity changes our view of . . .
    1. Wealth (Matthew 6:19, 20)
    2. Ethics (2 Corinthians 5:8)
    3. Accountability (Hebrews 9:27)
    4. Suffering (Romans 8:17)
    5. Success (Matthew 25:21).
C. Here is Jesus' final down-to-earth advice: "So do not worry
    . . . each day has enough trouble of its own" (6:31, 34). The
    past is gone. The future is not yet here. So live fully in this
    day God has given you and trust your future to God.

Facing Your Future With Faith

Text: Hebrews 12:2, 3

E veryone is interested in the future. This is evident in the wide-spread interest in astrology, psychic predictions, and Bible prophecy. What does the future hold? Will America continue to be the dominant superpower in the 21st century? Will Social Security be there when we need it? Will the stock market guarantee our financial future? Will the conflict in the Middle East lead us into World War III? Will Christ return in this generation?

Fritz R.S. Dressler, president of FRS Dressler and Associates, says, "Predicting the future is easy; it's trying to figure out what's going on now that's hard."

As believers, we turn to the Bible for our index on the future. God promises us a prophetic future based on the return of Christ (Titus 2:13; 1 Thessalonians 4:16-18; Revelation 11:15). We have one of two options: fear or faith (Luke 21:26, 28).

But there is more to our concern about the future than merely the prophetic side; there is also the personal side. When you look down the road of your own future—personally, family, church—what do you see? Are you full of hope and expectation? Or, are you filled with uncertainty and fear? God promises His people faith for the future. In

Christ, you can face your future with faith (Jeremiah 29:11; 33:3; Romans 4:18; Hebrews 11:8-10; 12:2; Philippians 3:13, 14). The watchword is "Press on!"

Press on—there's a . . .

- Heaven to be gained
- Hell to be shunned
- Reward to be received
- Dream to be fulfilled
- Finish line to be crossed
- Calling to be answered
- Enemy to be defeated
- Victory to be won
- Church to be built
- Harvest to be reaped
- World to be evangelized
- Kingdom to be established.

I. **Faith Sees the Possibilities (12:2).**
    A. *Jesus saw the joy set before Him.* Faith can envision the finished product before the work ever begins. What is the joy that is set before you . . . for your life . . . your marriage . . . your ministry?
    B. *You need a dream.* Martin Luther King Jr. stirred this nation with one clarion call: "I have a dream!" Joseph's brothers remarked, "Here comes that dreamer!" (Genesis 37:19). George Bernard Shaw said, "Some men see things and ask 'why?' I dream things that never were and ask 'why not?'" It is said of Jesus that in the company of sinners He dreamed of saints. What kind of dream do you need?
        1. *A God-given dream for your life* (Joel 2:28)
        2. *Realistic dreams.* Only realistic goals are attainable. Fantasy thinking is fatalistic. Maturity means possessing a realistic orientation toward life.

3. *A dream big enough to require faith* (Matthew 17:20;
   Hebrews 11:6). William Carey said, "Expect great
   things from God. Attempt great things for God."

The Power of Your Dream. Walter Fauntroy, former delegate to
the House of Representatives for the District of Columbia, delivered
a speech at Howard University, in which he said: "The past is yours,
learn from it. The present is yours, fulfill it. The future is yours, preserve it. Knowledge is yours, use it. Cancer is yours, cure it. Racism
is yours, end it. Do not be blinded by prejudice, disheartened by the
times or discouraged by the system. Do not let anything paralyze your
mind, tie your hands, or defeat your spirit. Take the world not to dominate it, but to deliver it; not to exploit it, but to enrich it—take the
dream and inherit the earth." (*The Executive Speechwriter Newsletter,*
Vol. 12, No. 3, Emerson Falls, St. Johnsbury, VT, p. 7).

Illustration

II. **Faith Pushes Through the Pain (v. 2).**
   A. Jesus endured the cross and scorned its shame. Two impor-
      tant statements are made here:
      1. *Jesus endured the cross.* He suffered the most intense
         pain imaginable to obtain our salvation. The word
         endure (hupomone, same as v. 1) means "active persist-
         ence toward one's goal as opposed to passive resigna-
         tion to trials."
      2. *Jesus scorned the shame of the cross.* Roman crucifixion
         was the height of humiliation. Horrible in its pain and dia-
         bolic in its humiliation—yet, Jesus scorned it. He count-
         ed the cost as nothing to pay for us. While we certainly
         cannot compare any sacrifice we make to that of our
         Lord's, He did leave us an example to follow. The price
         is a reality for any worthwhile endeavor. Many people
         never make their dreams come to pass because they can-
         not push through the pain and the difficulty. The writer to
         the Hebrews goes on to talk about the price (vv. 5-13).
   B. New endeavors are challenging and often painful, but
      push through the pain. Take the word *can't* out of your
      vocabulary.

Illustration

Overcoming Adversity. Ted Engstrom writes in his book, *The Pursuit of Excellence*:

- Cripple him, and you have a Sir Walter Scott.
- Put him in prison, and you have a John Bunyan.
- Bury him in the snow at Valley Forge, and you have a George Washington.
- Raise him in poverty, and you have an Abraham Lincoln.
- Strike him with paralysis, and you have a Franklin Roosevelt.
- Burn him so he'll never walk again, and you have the 1-mile record holder in 1934, Glenn Cunningham.
- Deafen him, and you have a Beethoven.
- Oppress him with racism, and you have a Booker T. Washington and a George Washington Carver.
- Call him a slow learner, and you have an Albert Einstein.

III. Faith Perseveres for the Prize (v. 2).

A. *Jesus sat down at the right hand of the throne of God.* Jesus sat down. He finished the work as our Great High Priest (Hebrews 4:14-16). *God's right hand* speaks of His power and the intercession of Jesus (Exodus 15:6; Matthew 22:41-46 [from Psalm 110:1]; Psalm 16:11). He prayed, "Father, I have glorified you on earth by finishing the work You gave Me to do" (see John 17:4).

B. *The believer's crown:* The incorruptible crown (1 Corinthians 9:25); the crown of righteousness (2 Timothy 4:8); the crown of life (James 1:12); the crown of glory (1 Peter 5:4). Jesus tells us, "Let no man take your crown" (see Revelation 3:11).

Stay Hungry! I remember watching a television interview with Arnold Schwarzeneggar conducted by Barbara Walters. He won the "Mr. Universe" title eight consecutive times and has gone on to a successful acting career. She asked him, "Do you have a philosophy of life?" He replied with a big smile, "Stay hungry."

Praise in the Valley

Text: 2 Chronicles 20:1-26

Someone sent me a card that read: "There's a secret to living life without worry, stress, disappointment and frustration." I opened the card and it continued, "Try to avoid becoming personally involved in your own life."

You get the point: As long as you live on this side of heaven, you will have to deal with life's tough moments. Life is a series of mountain peaks and valleys—great peak experiences and times of testing and trials. While we all wish life only involved the mountain peaks, we also know that we will pass through some valleys.

The Bible often describes tough times as a valley. David faced Goliath in the Valley of Elah (1 Samuel 17:19), and he also wrote of a place he called the "Valley of the Shadow" (see Psalm 23:4). Asaph described the "Valley of Baca [or Weeping]" (84:6). Ezekiel saw the spiritual desolation of Israel in his vision of the valley of dry bones (Ezekiel 37:1). And even the last of all human wars, the Battle of Armageddon (Revelation 16:16), is described as being waged in the "Valley of Decision" and the "Valley of Jehoshaphat" (Joel 3:2,

14). Isaiah described the messianic age as a time when "every valley shall be raised up" (Isaiah 40:4).

The challenge of faith is to turn every valley experience into a valley of praise. This is what the Old Testament King Jehoshaphat learned to do the day he received the news that three armies in an allied coalition had set their sights on destroying Jerusalem. The armies were marching up from the South to set up their offensive attack against the city.

The spiritual lessons he learned from that experience are invaluable for us as we face our own enemies. Before I get to that, let me introduce you to King Jehoshaphat. The name *Jehoshaphat* means "Jehovah has judged." He was a descendant of David who reigned over Judah from 872 to 848 B.C. (three of those years as co-regent with his father). His father, Asa, reigned as a righteous king, bringing much-needed spiritual reforms to Judah, including such acts as removing the high places and foreign altars and calling the people back to obedience to God. He even removed his own grandmother, Maacah, from her position as Queen Mother because she worshiped the Asherah pole. Unfortunately, in his last years, he acted foolishly by making a treaty with the king of Syria (Aram) instead of trusting in God. The result was war.

Jehoshaphat began ruling, along with his father, when he was 35. He walked upright before God, and God was with him (2 Chronicles 17:1-6). He commissioned the Levites to go throughout the towns of Judah teaching the Word of God (vv. 7-9). God established his kingdom, and the land enjoyed a time of peace. He was allied with the wicked Israeli King Ahab through marriage and was with him on the battlefield at Ramoth Gilead against the Syrians, where Ahab was killed.

When he returned to his palace, he was rebuked by Jehu the seer for assisting Ahab. In spite of his error in judgment, Jehoshaphat had set his heart on seeking God (19:3). All was well in the house and kingdom of Jehoshaphat. It was a time of peace and prosperity.

Then came the bad news.

Negativism. A woman had a parrot who always complained about everything. It was Thanksgiving Eve, and she was preparing the Thanksgiving meal. The parrot complained about everything as she worked. Finally, she had heard enough. She took him out of his cage and opened the refrigerator to punish him. "You'll stay in the refrigerator until you cool off and get control on your tongue," she said as she put him in and closed the door. The parrot was stunned. Shivering, he caught a glimpse of the Thanksgiving turkey, skinned, legs pointing upward from the pan. The parrot said to the turkey, "Good heavens, man! What did you say?"

Illustration

I. **The Predicament and the Panic (20:1-3a)**
   A. *Overwhelming odds without.* Israel faced three armies from Ammon, Moab and Mount Seir (Edom).
   B. *Fear and panic within.* The blessings of God do not exempt us from the adversities of life and spiritual attack (John 16:33; 1 Peter 5:8).

II. **The Prayer and the Prophecy (20:3b-21)**
   A. *The prayer principle.* Here's a prayer worth learning:
      1. *Rehearse your history of faith* (vv. 5, 6).
      2. *Remember God's promises in times of crisis* (vv. 7-9). This part of the prayer is taken from Solomon's dedication of the Temple in chapters 6 and 7.
   B. *Rely on God to do what you cannot do* (v. 12).
   C. *The prophecy* (which was based on Scripture) *proclaimed.* "Then the Spirit of the Lord came upon Jahaziel" (v. 14). A threefold admonition:
      1. Fear not; the battle is not yours, but God's (v. 15; see also Exodus 14:13, 14).
      2. "Stand firm and see the deliverance the Lord will give you" (v. 17).
      3. Go out and face the Enemy! (v. 17).
   D. *Prophecy received.* "Jehoshaphat bowed with his face to the ground . . . in worship before the Lord" (v. 18). Praise is an act of faith; it is faith in action. We, too, have to

receive God's Word by faith and act on it to see victory in our battles.

III. The Praise and the Victory (20:22-26)

A. *The power of faith.* "Have faith in the Lord your God and you will be upheld [and] be successful" (v. 20).

B. *The expression of faith.* He charged the worshipers to lead the army into battle. They sang the song used in the dedication of the Temple (5:13). The result is the entrance of God's glory in the Temple and on the battlefield. Note the charge to praise Him for "the splendor of his holiness" (20:21; also see Psalm 29:2). This means to praise Him for His holiness. We are also to dress in robes of holiness, spiritually speaking, as the priests wore.

C. *The reward of faith.* It took three days to gather the spoils. And the valley was named the Valley of Beracah, meaning "the valley of praise." God does more than we ask or even think possible if we trust Him (see Ephesians 3:20).

Fear Not—Only Believe

Text: Luke 8:40-56

During his 1933 Inaugural Address, President Franklin Roosevelt sought to calm a troubled America in the throes of depression by saying, "There is nothing to fear but fear itself." Fear is a feeling of dread, alarm, panic and anxiety. Fear ranges from mild anxiety to panic attacks. The Psychiatric Association has categorized a variety of phobias, such as acrophobia, claustrophobia, agoraphobia.

Research indicates that we are born with only two fears—the fear of falling and the fear of loud noises. All other fears are learned responses.

Fear takes on many forms—the fear of success, the fear of failure, the fear of rejection, the fear of disease, the fear of the future, the fear of life after death. Jesus described the last days as times of intense, worldwide fear (Luke 21:26).

Fear produces negative effects. Fear paralyzes decision making, immobilizes action, hinders prayer, limits faith, restricts relationships, lowers productivity, jeopardizes health, stifles joy.

Because of fear . . .

- Adam and Eve hid from God in the Garden (Genesis 3:8-10).
- Israel forfeited Canaan (Numbers 14:20-25).
- Ephraim turned back in the day of battle (Psalm 78:9).
- Saul's army fled from Goliath (1 Samuel 17:8-10).
- Gideon lost 22,000 of 32,000 fighting men (Judges 7:3).
- Elijah suffered depression (1 Kings 19:3-5).
- Jonah ran from the call of God (Jonah 1:3).
- The man with one talent buried it in the ground (Matthew 25:24).
- Christ's disciples cried out, "Master, do You not care that we perish?" (see Mark 4:38).
- Christ's disciples deserted Him at the cross (see Matthew 26:56).

In a world of fear, God speaks: "Fear not; only believe!" (see Luke 8:50). This was Christ's message to Jairus—"Fear not; only believe!" It's been said that fear is the distance between a man and God. Jairus was . . .

- A devout man—upstanding in the community; ruler of the synagogue. Synagogues developed after the Babylonian Exile were ruled largely by Pharisees, while Sadducees were in the Temple. Perhaps he had heard Jesus speak in his synagogue.
- A desperate man. When people get desperate, they get serious about God. He was willing to transcend his religious preju- dice even to the point of going to Jesus.
- A disillusioned man. He receives the worst news: "Your daugh- ter is dead." He is down, his faith disappointed, his hope gone.

Jesus spoke four profound, life-changing words: "Fear not; only believe!"

Fear Not . . . Jesus Is With You. A little girl was awakened by the loud burst of thunder and the flash of lightning. She jumped out of bed and ran across the house to her parents' bedroom. "I want to get in bed with you and Dad," she told her mother. "Now sweetheart," her mother responded, "there's nothing to be afraid of. It's just a storm. Now go back to bed. Nothing will harm you. Besides, Jesus is in your room with you. He'll take care of you." The little girl wouldn't move. She said, "Mother, you go in there and sleep with Jesus. I'm sleeping in here with Dad!"

Illustration

THE PRINCIPLES LEARNED
FROM THIS ACCOUNT

I. **Accept the Validity of God's Promises.**

    A. At times, we focus more on the circumstances than God's promises. Looking at circumstances can cause fear, like Peter looking at the water when he tried to walk on it. He sank when he took his eyes off Jesus. When we keep our minds focused on God and His promises, we have faith, and that faith gives us perfect peace (see Isaiah 26:3).

An astronaut was about to enter the spacecraft. A news reporter asked him, "How do you feel about the mission you're about to take?" The astronaut replied, "How would you feel knowing that this spacecraft consisted of 140,000 parts, each supplied by the lowest bidder?" Now that's the kind of anxiety we feel when we look only at the circumstances.

Illustration

    B. The promises of God are described in Scripture as . . .

        1. Unfailing (1 Kings 8:56)

        2. Assured (Romans 4:21)

        3. Grounded in Christ (2 Corinthians 1:20)

        4. Great and precious (2 Peter 1:4)

        5. Everlasting (1 John 2:25).

Illustration

Faith Through the Word. D.L. Moody said that he used to pray
for faith. Then he read Romans 10:17: "Faith comes by hearing, and
hearing by the word of God" (*NKJV*). Meditating on Scripture will
fill our hearts with the promises of God, which become the source
and power of faith.

II. Commit the Outcome to God.

Fear anticipates the worst possible outcome. Fear haunts us with
the question "What if?" What if you fail? What if your health
fails? What if you lose your job? What if the economy goes
sour? *Fear* can be defined as "False Expectations Appearing
Real." But faith knows our lives are in the hands of God. You've
got to answer the question "What if?" with "I know!" Paul said,
"I know whom I have believed and am persuaded that He is able
. . ." (2 Timothy 1:12, *NKJV*). Remember the promise of God
in Deuteronomy 33:27: "The eternal God is your refuge, and
underneath are the everlasting arms."

A. Examples of those who trusted the outcome of their crisis
   to God:
   1. Job in his suffering (Job 13:15)
   2. Shadrach, Meshach and Abednego facing death (Daniel
      3:16-18)
   3. Paul in prison (2 Timothy 4:6-8, 18)

B. The prayer of Jewish children at night: "Father, into Your
   hands I commit my spirit" (see Luke 23:46). This was how
   Christ faced the cross. What or whom do you need to commit into the hands of God? Pray, "Father, into Your hands
   I commit _____." You fill in the blank.

III. Don't Doubt in the Dark What God Has Shown You in the Light.

This is Corrie ten Boom's definition of faith. Jairus had to deal
with the divine delay (see Psalm 130:5, 6; Habakkuk 2:3). We,
too, have to learn to wait on the fulfillment of God's Word. Fear
sets in during the delay period between the promise given and
the promise fulfilled. Jesus told Jairus that He would heal his
daughter, and nothing was going to change that fact. Note other

Biblical examples of those who waited on God in faith during periods of delay:

A. Abraham waited 10 years for Isaac to be born, then was tested by God at Mount Moriah.

B. Joseph waited 12 years in prison before his dream was fulfilled.

C. Joshua and Caleb waited 40 years in the desert because of the unbelief of their generation, but they lived to possess the Promised Land.

D. David waited for 10 years, being hounded by King Saul in the desert, before he was crowned king. As a fugitive on the run, he wrote: "The Lord is my light and my salvation—whom shall I fear?" (Psalm 27:1).

E. The disciples waited 10 days in the Temple courts for the Spirit, who came with power on the Day of Pentecost. Remember the adage: "Fear knocked at the door. Faith answered, and there was no one there."

Contentment in an Age of Consumerism

Text: Hebrews 13:5, 6

A number of years ago, singer Paul Simon wrote a song titled "American Tune." In it, he sings the line "I don't have a friend who feels at ease." He put his finger on the problem of discontentment.

Consumerism robs us of contentment. Consumerism convinces us that happiness is based on how much "stuff" we have. It sells us on the idea that bigger is better. It clutters our landscape with neon signs and overpowering billboards telling us that what we need to be happy is *more*. Consumerism motivates the average American family to spend 115 percent of their income, leaving the nation buried under a pile of debt and spiraling bankruptcies.

God calls us to *contentment*, which means "not inclined to complain or desire something else; satisfied; submissive to circumstances; freedom from worry or unsatisfied desires." The difference between the contented person and the discontented person is not how many possessions they own, but whether or not they enjoy what they have. Let's clear up a basic misunderstanding: Contentment does not mean to maintain the status quo, to settle for second best, or to turn down opportunities to better ourselves and our lifestyles. To the contrary, we are called to press on, to rise up to our potential, and to accomplish great things for the glory of God. But we keep our ambitions in check as we experience a sense of fulfillment, peace and joy—regardless of our situation in life.

The Bible teaches contentment. Proverbs 15:16 says, "Better a little with the fear of the Lord than great wealth with turmoil" (see also Philippians 4:11; 1 Timothy 6:6, 8; Hebrews 13:5, 6).

Illustration

Christmas Shopping. I heard recently about a man who was Christmas-shopping in a department store. He noticed a weird-looking gadget, but he couldn't figure out what it was. So he asked the saleslady what it was designed to do. She replied, "It doesn't do anything, it's just a Christmas gift."

This passage in Hebrews also teaches us valuable lessons about how to cultivate contentment.

I. **Never Measure Your Worth by Your Wealth (v. 5a).**
    A. *The money factor.* The Bible has a lot to say about money. In fact, there are over 2,000 verses that deal with money in one way or another.
        1. Money is fundamental to life (Ecclesiastes 10:19).˙
        2. Money is neither good nor bad in itself.
        3. Money is entrusted to us by God (Proverbs 3:9).
        4. Money is inseparably connected to our spiritual growth (Matthew 6:21).
        5. Money makes a great servant but a terrible master (Ecclesiastes 5:10: "Whoever loves money never has money enough; whoever loves wealth is never satisfied with his income").
        6. God will bless us financially (see 3 John 2).
        7. Money must be given in order to achieve financial peace and divine blessings (Malachi 3:9, 10).

Determined to "take it with him" when he died, a very wealthy man prayed until finally the Lord gave in. There was only one condition: he could bring only one suitcase of his wealth. He decided to fill the case with gold bullion. Finally, the day came when the Lord called him home. Saint Peter greeted him at the pearly gate but told him he couldn't bring his suitcase. "Oh, but I have an agreement with God," the man explained. "That's unusual," said Peter. "Mind if I take a look?" The man opened the suitcase to reveal the shining gold bullion. Saint Peter was amazed and asked the man, "Why in the world would you bring pavement?" (*Reader's Digest*, contributed by Reverend Warren Keating in *The Joyful Noiseletter,* December 1995, p. 64).

Illustration

B. *Keep your lives free from the love of money.* Someone said, "You write your autobiography in your checkbook." The love of money is not wealth. Abraham, Job, David, Solomon, Joseph and Moses were all wealthy men. Lydia was a wealthy businesswoman who helped support Paul's ministry. The love of money is the measure of our worth by possessions. But your worth is measured by the value God places on your life as His child.

II. **Enjoy What You Have and Where You Are Today (5b).**
   A. *Contentment* means "experiencing joy today." Sure, you have goals for tomorrow. Dream big dreams and go for them with all your heart, but stop and smell the flowers along the way. Stay off the fast tract. The only thing ahead of you is your funeral, so slow down. Here's a quote you'll enjoy: "The happiest people don't necessarily have the best of everything; they just make the best of everything." It's the old "Bloom where you're planted" principle.

Once while Francis of Assisi was hoeing his garden, he was asked, "What would you do if you were suddenly to learn that you were to die at sunset today?" He replied, "I would finish hoeing my garden."

Illustration

B. *The danger of discontentment.* Discontentment leads to covetousness, which comes in two forms:
   1. Jealousy of others
   2. Resentment toward others. *Covetousness comes from a Greek word meaning "grasping for more."* Tim Kimmel says that covetousness is "material inebriation. It's an addiction to things that don't last and a craving for things that don't really matter." Discontentment complains, "If only."
      a. If only I had a job . . . a better job . . . a more understanding boss . . . enough money to retire on . . . a bigger house . . . a thinner waist . . . a better education . . . a husband . . . a different husband . . . a child . . . a lifestyle like . . .
      b. If only I hadn't dropped out of school . . . been forced to get married . . . had an abortion . . . started drinking . . . been fired . . . run up so many debts . . . neglected my wife . . . quit that job . . . sold that stock.
      c. If only they had given me more playing time . . . recognized my potential . . . offered me the job . . . encouraged me in my sports . . . been honest with me . . . stuck with me.
      d. If only they hadn't abandoned me as a baby . . . discouraged me . . . prejudged me . . . pushed me so hard to achieve . . . lied to me . . . been so interested in making money . . . been ashamed of my handicap.
      e. If only . . . if only . . . if only. (Tim Kimmel, "Robbed of Rest," *Focus on the Family*, Feb. 1988, pp. 2-5.)

Illustration

Charles Boswell, former football star at the University of Alabama, held high hopes of a professional football career. However, he lost his eyesight in combat during World War II. Later, he went on to become the National Blind Golf Champion 17 times. He said, "I never count what I've lost. I only count what I have left."

III. Derive Your Happiness From Your Relationship to Christ, Not Your Life Situation (v. 6).

The apostle Paul showed us the way to contentment in Christ (Philippians 4:11). What was the secret of the sufficiency of Christ? Joy is mentioned 16 times in this letter, and Jesus is referred to some 50 times. Jesus is our . . .

- Purpose for life (1:21)
- Pattern for life (2:5)
- Passion in life (3:10)
- Prize for life (v. 14)
- Power for life (4:13).

Here is the Japanese version of Psalm 23:

> The Lord is my pacesetter, I shall not rush.
>
> He makes me stop and rest for quiet intervals,
>
> He provides me with images of stillness which deepen my serenity.
>
> He leads me in ways of efficiency through calmness of mind,
>
> And His guidance is peace.
>
> Even though I have a great many things to accomplish each day,
>
> I will not fret, for His presence is here.
>
> His timelessness, His all-importance will keep me in balance.
>
> He prepares refreshment and renewal in the midst of my activity.
>
> By anointing my mind with oils of tranquillity
>
> My cup of joyous energy overflows.
>
> Surely harmony and effectiveness shall be the fruits of my hours.
>
> For I shall walk in the pace of the Lord,
>
> And dwell in His house forever.

Illustration

Have You Heard From God Lately?

Text: Isaiah 30:19-21

Does God speak to people today? We know He spoke in times past. There is no way to read the Bible and not hear God speaking. God spoke the worlds into existence. God spoke to Abraham to go to the Land of Promise. God spoke to Moses and gave him His Law. God spoke to Belshazzar with the handwriting on the wall. God spoke to Paul on the Damascus road. God spoke to the apostles and gave them the Scripture.

But can we actually hear from God? Or, is hearing from God only for the superspiritual or, even worse, for the emotionally unstable? Let's be honest—some people who claim to hear from God cause us great concern.

The voice of God can be seen from a universal and personal standpoint. Universally, God speaks through creation (Psalm 19:1), Christ (Hebrews 1:1, 2), and conscience.

God also speaks personally. This completes the loop of prayer. According to a *Newsweek* survey, 54 percent of adults said that they pray every day (29 percent more than once a day). Eighty-seven percent said that they believe God answers their prayers at least some of the time. The question is, does God speak back to us? (Kenneth L. Woodward, "Is God Listening?" *Newsweek,* March 31, 1997).

God promises to speak to us: "Your ears will hear a voice behind you, saying, 'This is the way; walk in it'" (Isaiah 30:21). Jesus said, "My sheep hear My voice" (John 10:27, *NKJV*).

HOW DOES GOD SPEAK?

I.   God Speaks Through Scripture.

A.   God speaks through the personal application of His Word. You won't necessarily find out about whether or not you should take that job, or whom you're going to marry, but you will meet God. He will speak to you about Himself.

B.   We must exercise caution that we rightly divide the Word of Truth and do not read things into Scripture that are not what God intended. This happens often when we want to convince ourselves we are right, so we look for something in the Bible to confirm our biases. It also happens in Biblical teaching where analogies and types are taken from Biblical stories and applied to issues today when, in reality, God never intended those analogies to be made. There is a great deal of hype today about end-time prophecy and the return of Christ that is not stated in Scripture but is simply from ministers reading things into the Bible.

C.   The more frequently you read the Bible, the more clearly you will hear the voice of God directing you and giving you wisdom for decision making. "From infancy you have known the holy Scriptures which are able to make you wise" (2 Timothy 3:15).

II. God Speaks Through Life Situations.

"In all things God works . . ." (Romans 8:28). C.S. Lewis said, "God whispers in our pleasure, He shouts in our pain."

Illustration

George Washington Carver was a devout Christian. He maintained daily devotions, usually beginning his prayer with the word *behold!* The theme of his devotions was, "Behold! What will God show me?" It was his way of opening his mind to God's Word and to his world. One day he was holding a sweet potato. God said to him, "Behold! What can you do with it?" Today if you visit Tuskegee Institute in Alabama, you can see samples of the 118 things that Dr. Carver did with the sweet potato. He saw the creation from a new perspective, and in doing so, unlocked some of God's secrets.

III. God Speaks Through Signs.

God gives dreams, visions and spiritual gifts to speak to His people (Joel 2:28, 29; Acts 13:2; Hebrews 2:4). The acid test of such experiences is that they must be confirmed by Scripture.

IV. God Speaks Through Significant People.

There is safety and success through wise counselors (Proverbs 11:14). There are different types of counsel we need:

A.   Word of counsel for encouragement

B.   Word of correction to get us back on track

C.   Word of comfort to give us new strength and joy

D.   Word of confirmation to let us know we are in the will of God

V. God Speaks in the Sanctuary of the Soul (Psalm 73:16, 17).

A.   The Elijah experience: We, too, look for God in the earthquake, fire, wind. God is usually in the gentle whisper, the still small voice (1 Kings 19:12).

B.   The result of God's Word is always peace (Colossians 3:15). The peace of God ruling in our hearts is the greatest evidence that we are hearing from God.

C.   So, what do we need to do in order to hear God when He speaks?

1.   *Tune in.* During Jesus' last week in Jerusalem before His death, He prayed in a public area, "Father, glorify your name!" Then God spoke from heaven: "'I have

glorified it, and will glorify it again.' The crowd that was there . . . said it had thundered; others said an angel had spoken to him" (John 12:28, 29). They only heard thunder. They were out of tune. Do we hear only thunder, or do we hear God speaking?

2. *Check it out.* Make sure that every word you hear, especially from others and those who claim to have a prophecy for you, is in harmony with Scripture.

3. *Do it!* When God speaks, obey. "Whatever He says to you, do it" (John 2:5, *NKJV*). Hearing and obeying are inseparably connected (Luke 11:28; James 1:22).

When Hope Fades

Text: Jeremiah 33:1-3

If you were an artist and decided to paint a picture to best portray the meaning of hope, what would you paint? Years ago an artist named Watts titled one of his paintings, "Hope." It shows a woman sitting on a world that had treated her most unfairly. Her eyes are bandaged, preventing her from seeing her way ahead. In her hands she held a harp with all the strings broken except one. Triumphantly, she strikes that last string, and from it a beautiful melody lifts from the harp over her world and fills her dark night with stars.

In the midst of a broken world, God gives us a harp with a string called *hope*. When we radiate hope, we fill our hearts, our homes and our world with the triumphant spirit of praise that declares, "With God all things are possible."

What a tragedy to lose hope. In America today, the second leading cause of death among teenagers is suicide—no hope. Our urban centers are steeped in an endless cycle of violence and poverty—no hope. Eighty percent of children born in some inner cities are born to unwed mothers. Overall, the rate is 30 percent. Some 17.6 million

Americans suffer from depression—costing an estimated $23.8 billion in lost work and productivity and $12.4 billion in treatment costs (*U.S. News and World Report,* Dec. 9, 1996, p. 17).

Yet, God gives hope. Hope is a confident expectation based on certain fundamental truths and actions. Hebrews 6:19 reads: "We have this hope as an anchor for the soul."

In his difficult circumstances Jeremiah learned three things about God that gave him hope.

I.   The God of New Beginnings (v. 1)

    A. *The historical setting.* Jerusalem was under seige (587 B.C.), and Jeremiah was imprisoned by Zedekiah for his prophecies about God's judgment on the nation. The king and the elders still consulted him.

    B. *The word of hope.* Note the phrase "a second time." This was similar to the earlier word about the field to purchase (32:1-15). He put the signed deed in a jar to be preserved as a sign of hope. A new beginning was at hand (33:4-9). Zedekiah's efforts to save the nation would fail. God's promise to heal and restore would be fulfilled. The word came while Jeremiah was in prison. The adversity could not hinder the word of God from coming to Jeremiah or from being fulfilled about Judah's restoration. As Paul said, "The word of God is not chained" (2 Timothy 2:9, *NKJV*).

    C. *The God of new beginnings* (Isaiah 43:18, 19).

Illustration

Karl Downs. If I were to mention the name Karl Downs, probably no one has ever heard of him. He was a Methodist preacher in Oakland, California, who died of a heart attack when he was still quite young. Several years before he died, he was asked by the Juvenile Court to take responsibility for a young man who was always getting into trouble. Karl Downs accepted the responsibility and became a father to this young man. While you may not know who Karl Downs is, you know who the young boy is—Jackie Robinson. But there would probably have never been a Jackie Robinson if there hadn't been a Karl Downs.

II. The God Who Makes All Things Possible (v. 2)

The Army Corps of Engineers have a slogan: "The difficult we do immediately; the impossible takes a little longer."

A. The restoration of Jerusalem appeared to be impossible— but possible when based on the power of God (v. 2; 32:17). God asks, "Is there anything too hard for Me?" (32:27, *NKJV*).

B. Human history is the record of God making the impossible possible.
   1. Impossibility of the Creation (Genesis 1:1)
   2. Impossibility of the Incarnation (Matthew 1:23)
   3. Impossibility of miracles (John 14:12)
   4. Impossibility of salvation (Romans 5:8)
   5. Impossibility of resurrection (Matthew 28:6)

Testimony of Terrell Brandon. In February 1997, all-star guard for the Cleveland Cavaliers Terrell Brandon shared the testimony of his mother's healing on an ESPN interview. In 1993 she was diagnosed with terminal cancer of the liver and sent home. The doctors had done all they could. The interviewer asked, "What happened?" Brandon shared that his parents are people of faith and that the church prayed fervently. The next diagnosis showed no signs of cancer. The interviewer asked, "So the cancer disappeared without any explanation?" No, there is an explanation—Isaiah 53:5: "By His stripes we are healed" (*NKJV*).

Illustration

III. The God Who Answers Prayer (v. 3)

A. God told Jeremiah, "Call to me . . ."

B. What an invitation—to call on God personally (Psalm 18:3)!

C. What a privilege to pray (Hebrews 10:19-22)!

D. What a responsibility to pray for others (James 5:16)!

E. "I will answer you." God answers prayer according to . . .
   1. His will (1 John 5:14, 15)
   2. Our faith (Matthew 9:29; Mark 11:24; Hebrews 11:6)
   3. His infinite resources (Philippians 4:19; Ephesians 3:20).

F. "I will . . . tell you great and unsearchable things." The word *unsearchable* in Hebrew, *bashur*, means "inaccessible; beyond the grasp of human knowledge." The word is used of the fortified cities of Canaan (Deuteronomy 1:28: "walled up," KJV). God promises to reveal hidden things to us by His Spirit (1 Corinthians 2:9, 10).

The Throne of Grace

Text: Hebrews 4:14-16

If I were to ask you what is the root cause of all human suffering, what would you answer? The Bible tells us clearly that the root cause of our suffering—in spirit, mind and body—is our alienation from God.

Augustine put his finger on it in his prayer, "Our hearts were made for Thee, O God, and they shall not rest until they rest in Thee." Goethe added, "All human longing is really the longing for God." The rock group Dishwalla sings, "Tell me all your thoughts on God, 'cause I would really like to meet Him." Paul says, "Once you were alienated from God . . ." (Colossians 1:21).

In the beginning Adam and Eve experienced unbroken communion with God. Then they sinned. The result was alienation from God—separation from God. A great gulf was fixed between us and God.

But God had a remedy—a bridge to cross the chasm caused by our sin so that we could be reconciled to Him. That remedy was a Priest. The Latin word for *priest* is *pontifex,* which means "a bridge-builder."

The first prophecy given in Scripture concerning this Priest is in Genesis 3:15. God illustrated the work of our Priest when He made coverings for Adam and Eve to cover their shame—symbolic of the Atonement, which means "to cover."

Jesus did not come into this world simply to . . .

- Preach, "Repent, for the kingdom of heaven is at hand" (Matthew 4:17, *NKJV*)
- Deliver the Sermon on the Mount
- Confront the ritualism and tradition
- Teach us the way of love
- Heal the sick, feed the multitude, cast out demons, raise the dead, or to prophesy concerning God's work in history.

He came as our Great High Priest to atone for our sins that we might be reconciled to God (Luke 10:19; Mark 10:45; John 1:29; Romans 5:8; 2 Corinthians 5:21).

What makes the Christian experience different from the religions of the world is the fact that we don't merely follow one who is a teacher, a prophet, a moral example, a benefactor, or a philosopher. We follow the One who came as God's priest for the world. As the writer of Hebrews tells us, "Seeing then that we have a great High Priest . . ." (4:14, *NKJV*).

While many facets of this passage could be investigated for their deep spiritual riches, I want to focus on God's invitation to us to come boldly to the throne of grace because we have a Great High Priest. Here we see the benefits of His priesthood.

I. **What Is the Throne of Grace?**
    A. *The throne of God* (Psalm 103:19; Isaiah 6:1; Revelation 4:2; 20:11).
    B. *The cover of the ark of the covenant—called the mercy seat.*
       1. Design: solid gold; two cherubim (Genesis 3:24; Psalm 99:1)
       2. Purpose: place where the atonement blood was sprinkled

C. *The Incarnation and indwelling of Christ.* The fact that the throne of God and the mercy seat are one reveals that God has established His throne in the midst of humanity. The Tabernacle represented the incarnation of Christ and finally, our hearts. Thus Jesus preached, "Repent, for the kingdom of heaven is at hand" (Matthew 4:17, *NKJV*) and said the locale of that Kingdom is within (Luke 17:20, 21).

II. **How Should We Approach the Throne?**
   A. *The confidence. Boldly* does not mean casually or without reverence, but literally means "saying all." That is to utterly and completely express one's thoughts, feelings, and sins to God; holding nothing back; refusing to play games with God. The Hebrews writer tells us that God has given us spiritual first-amendment rights of free speech before His throne. This invitation stands in contrast with the economy of the Old Testament. Only the high priest entered the Holy of Holies to stand before the ark of the covenant. An inner veil kept the ark hidden from the sight of the priests as they ministered daily in the next room—the Holy Place. You can be honest because God understands (Hebrews 4:15).
   B. *The basis: We have a Great (superior) High Priest.* What makes Him great?
      1. *The person of Jesus.* He has (1) passed through the heavens. In the words of Christina Rossetti, "Heaven cannot hold Him." He is greater than the heavens—than all the angelic hosts and the vast universe itself. He has ascended to the highest heaven as Lord above all. His exaltation to the right hand of God is in view (Philippians 2:9-11). He is (2) the Son of God (mentioned 49 times in Scripture).
      2. *The provision of Jesus* (Hebrews 4:15). The writer brings into view Christ's humanity, which refers to His death (10:19-22).
      3. Jesus fulfills the Old Testament priesthood of Aaron and the Levites:

AARON: THE PATTERN	JESUS: THE PERFECTION
Entered earthly tabernacle	Entered heaven itself
Entered once a year	Entered once for all
Went behind the veil	Rent the veil in two
Offered sacrifice for his own sins	Offered Himself for our sins
Offered sacrifice once a year	Offered Himself once for all
Offered the blood of bulls and goats	Offered His own blood

IN THE LEVITICAL SYSTEM	IN CHRIST
Consecration was temporal	Consecration is eternal
Priests were fallible	Priest is sinless
Priesthood was changing	Priesthood is changeless
Ministry was continual	Ministry is final
Sacrifices were insufficient	Sacrifice is all-sufficient
Intercession was not prevailing	Intercession is all-prevailing

4. *The superiority of Christ's priesthood.*
   a. He has no need of the priestly garments.
   b. He has no need of the sacrifices.
   c. He has no need of the festivals.
   d. He has obtained a more excellent way.
   e. He has a better covenant . . . promises . . . sacrifice
    . . . priesthood . . . mediation . . . resurrection.

III. What Is Provided for Us at the Throne?
   A. *Mercy: Love in action.* The Bible says that God's anger lasts only for a moment (Psalm 30:5), but "his love endures forever" (100:5).

Illustration

I met a young woman after a service who told me, "I never feel I measure up to God's standards." Then she asked, "What can I do to really grasp the love of God for me?" The answer for that is to go to the throne and see the nail-pierced hands of the Son of God for you and hear God say, "You are My beloved son/daughter. With you I am well pleased."

B. *Grace to help in the time of need.* This means to "receive timely grace." *Grace* means "to give freely":

God's
Riches
At
Christ's
Expense.

C. Grace is God moving toward us out of His own initiative; God doing for us what we cannot do for ourselves; God paying a debt for us that we could never pay; God acting toward us in ways we do not deserve. God has grace for every need. "And God is able to make all grace abound to you, so that in all things at all times, having all that you need, you will abound in every good work" (2 Corinthians 9:8).

Issues of the Heart

Text: Proverbs 4:23

The human heart is an amazing organ. Your heart—a hollow muscle about the size of your fist and weighing between 8 and 12 ounces—is the body's "perpetual motion system." It supplies blood to the body systems through its own circulatory system, which is between 60 and 100 miles long including 50 feet of arteries and veins and 62,000 miles of capillaries.

The heart pumps on average 5 quarts of blood per minute—2,000 gallons per day. During times of exertion—like running—the heart will pump up to 40 quarts a minute, responding to an immediate demand made by the muscles. Because of their regular, strenuous activity, runners and swimmers frequently have enlarged hearts.

A normal adult heart pumps at a rate of 70 to 75 times per minute and beats 42,000 times an hour, 36 million times a year, and more than 2 1/2 billion times in a lifetime.

As tough and endurable as the heart is, however, it must be maintained with utmost care. Heart disease is the number one cause of death in the United States. Over 22 million Americans suffer from heart disease, of which almost 700,000 people die every year. (National Center for Health Statistics, 2003 information). We also have a spiritual heart. From a Biblical perspective, the heart represents one's spiritual, mental and moral self; the sense of intellect, will and emotions; the central part of the human personality; the essence of one's being. We talk about "the heart of the matter" or "the heart of the sea"; it is the true person, including both motives and morals, emotions and thoughts. The apostle Peter speaks of the "hidden man of the heart" (1 Peter 3:4, KJV). There is a cure for spiritual heart disease. God promises us a new heart (Ezekiel 36:26). Look at how the Bible describes the conditions of a heart that is turned toward God:

- 2 Chronicles 11:16: "Those from every tribe of Israel who set their hearts on seeking the Lord."
- Nehemiah 9:8: "You found his heart faithful to you, and you made a covenant with him [Abraham]."
- Psalm 57:7: "My heart is steadfast, O God, my heart is steadfast."
- Jeremiah 31:33, 34: Obedient heart
- Acts 4:32: One in heart
- 2 Corinthians 4:16: Courageous heart
- Ephesians 1:18: Enlightened heart
- Ephesians 6:6: Dedicated heart
- Colossians 3:1, 23: Diligent heart

I. **Examine Your Heart (Psalm 19:14; 139:23, 24; 2 Corinthians 13:5).**

    A. Only the Holy Spirit can reveal what is in our hearts so that we can walk with God in fellowship and have no barriers between us and God.

    B. Check your motives. Plato said, "The unexamined life is not worth living."

II. **Purify Your Heart (Psalm 24:3-5; Matthew 5:8; James 4:8; 1 Peter 1:22).**

    A. Without cleansing, our hearts become hardened. Hebrews

3:12, 13: "See to it, brothers, that none of you has a sinful, unbelieving heart that turns away from the living God. But encourage one another daily, as long as it is called Today, so that none of you will be hardened by sin's deceitfulness."

B. This is what God promises to do with our sins:
1. Forgive our sins (1 John 1:9)
2. Cast them into the sea (Micah 7:19)
3. Take them away (Isaiah 6:7)
4. Cover them (Psalm 32:1)
5. Wipe them out (Acts 3:19)
6. Remember them no more (Hebrews 8:12)
7. Remove them as far as the east is from the west (Psalm 103:12)

III. **Turn Your Heart (Joel 2:12; Malachi 4:5, 6).**

We need to "set [our] hearts on things above . . . not on earthly things" (Colossians 3:1, 2).

A. Reassess your priorities and values because the heart can be misguided, misdirected.

B. Here are some misplaced affections seen in Biblical examples:
1. Cain set his heart on pride and murdered his brother.
2. Esau set his heart on temporary pleasure and forfeited his inheritance.
3. Lot set his heart on Sodom and lost his family.
4. King Saul set his heart on political power and lost the throne.
5. David set his heart on Bathsheba and sinned against God.
6. Solomon set his heart on foreign wives and turned his heart against God.
7. Judas set his heart on personal gain and betrayed Christ.
8. The rich young ruler set his heart on material possessions and rejected the kingdom of God.
9. Demas set his heart on the world and forsook the ministry.

IV. Strengthen Your Heart (Ephesians 3:16, 17).

Nourish, strengthen, exercise your spiritual heart. "Be strong in the Lord and in his mighty power" (6:10). "Build yourselves up in your most holy faith" (Jude 20). Just as diet has a tremendous effect upon the condition of the heart, spiritual diet affects the spiritual heart. We need a diet of worship, prayer and reading of Scripture, and a life of service to others in order to be strong spiritually.

V. Quieten Your Heart (Psalm 112:7, 8).

This passage says, "He will have no fear of bad news; his heart is steadfast, trusting in the Lord. His heart is secure, he will have no fear; in the end he will look in triumph on his foes." The heart gets troubled by guilt and fear (Luke 21:26). Heart disease is often stress-related in nature. Only grace can give us a clean heart free from guilt and fear. If you want peace of mind . . .

A. *Commit your life to Christ* (Romans 10:9, 10). Bishop Ryle said, "One thief on the cross was saved, that none should despair; and only one, that none should presume."

B. *Commit your concerns to Christ* (1 Peter 5:7).

The noted British preacher Caesar Milan attended a banquet in London one evening for special dignitaries. A young lady sang for the gathering. After her singing, he had the opportunity to meet her. He said, "As you sang, I couldn't help thinking what you could accomplish for God if you dedicated yourself and your gift fully to Him." She was offended by his remark and proceeded to tell him so. "I didn't mean to offend you, but I hope you will prayerfully consider what I said." That night she was restless, waking up off and on, troubled by the conviction of the Holy Spirit. At 2 a.m. she got out of bed, bowed her knees and dedicated herself to God. That night she penned the words of this song:

Just as I am, without one plea,
But that Thy blood was shed for me,
And that Thou bidd'st me come to Thee,
O Lamb of God, I come!
—Charlotte Elliott

Illustration

Back to Babylon

Text: Daniel 1:1-8

The year was 605 B.C.. The Babylonian army surrounded the city of Jerusalem. King Jehoiakim surrendered without a fight. Judah then came under the control of Babylon. Nebuchadnezzar carried some of the holy articles of the Temple, along with a number of the royal family and nobility, back to Babylon. Among these exiles was the now-famous personality—Daniel.

The Babylonian army returned again in 597 B.C. to take away more captives. And finally in 586 B.C., they destroyed Jerusalem, along with its Temple, and exiled the entire nation as slaves to Babylon. Now in exile, the people were dejected and hopeless. The psalmist laments their distress in Psalm 137.

Throughout Scripture, Babylon is a symbol of evil. Today the spirit of Babylon is alive in our midst. The word *babel* means "confusion." Babylon is mentioned in Revelation 14:8 as "great." The city first appears in Genesis 10:10 and 11:9 and represents human systems of politics, religion and commerce in rebellion to God. Babylon reflects the pride of man, which seeks to build the city of man without the city of God. Early Christians referred to Rome as

Babylon. The Revelator announces that Babylon is "fallen!" (14:8). The Greek aorist tense is used to denote completed action. The imminence and certainty of Babylon's destruction is in view.

When we look around at the conditions of America today, we feel something like the Israelites must have felt when they were exiled to Babylon. We, too, are asking, "How can we sing the songs of the Lord while in a foreign land?" (Psalm 137:4). How can we live as the covenant people of God in a ungodly world?

Our roots are distinctively Judeo-Christian. Our laws are based on the moral absolutes found in Scripture. John Adams said, "The highest glory of the American Revolution was this: It connected in one indissoluble bond the principles of civil government with the principles of Christianity." As Christopher Dawson observed: "Christianity is the soul of Western civilization. When the soul is gone, the body putrefies."

We are asking the same question the Israelites asked in Babylon: "How should we then live?" (Ezekiel 33:10, KJV). What we need is to recapture the spirit of Daniel: "Daniel resolved not to defile himself" (Daniel 1:8).

We affirm with Joshua, "As for me and my household, we will serve the Lord" (Joshua 24:15). We declare with David, "The Lord is my light and my salvation—whom shall I fear?" (Psalm 27:1). We pray with Christ, "Not my will, but yours be done" (Luke 22:42). We declare with Paul, "For to me, to live is Christ and to die is gain" (Philippians 1:21). We affirm with Peter, "Make your calling and election sure. For if you do these things, you will never fall" (2 Peter 1:10).

Daniel gives us three lessons for life.

I.   **Remember Who You Are.**

　　A. Name change: *Daniel* means "God is my judge." His name was changed to *Belteshazzar*, "prince of Bel," the chief Babylonian deity. Yet, 75 times he refers to himself as Daniel in his writings. He held on to his sense of identity. The television series *Roots* was important to a number of people because it helped recapture a sense of identity. Eric Erickson said that the greatest crisis everyone faces is the identity crisis. Identity is derived from the way in which we answer four questions:

1. Who am I?
2. Where did I come from?
3. Where am I going?
4. Why am I here?

Christian Hertner was running hard for a second term in office. One day after a busy morning and no lunch, he arrived at a church barbecue. Hertner was famished. As the governor moved down the serving line, he held out his plate to the woman serving chicken. She put one piece on his plate and turned to the next person in line. "Excuse me," Governor Hertner said, "Do you mind if I have another piece of chicken?" "Sorry, only one to a customer," said the woman." The governor was a modest man, but he was also hungry, so he decided to throw a little weight around. "Lady, do you know who I am?" he said. "I am the governor of this state." "Do you know who I am?" the woman responded. "I'm the lady in charge of the chicken. Now move along, Mister!"

Illustration

B.   *Spiritual Identity.* We all have (1) a personal identity, (2) a family identity, (3) an ethnic identity and (4) a cultural identity (we like different kinds of music, etc.). But most importantly, we have a spiritual identity. Who are we?

1. Sons and daughters (John 1:12)
2. Heirs and joint-heirs (Romans 8:15, 16)
3. God's masterpiece of creation (Psalm 8:4-7)
4. God's treasured possession (Malachi 3:17)
5. The apple of God's eye (Deuteronomy 32:10)
6. The temple of the Holy Spirit (1 Corinthians 6:19)
7. The friends of God (John 15:15)
8. A royal priesthood (1 Peter 2:9, 10)
9. Overcomers (1 John 2:14; 4:4; 5:4)

C.   Identity determines destiny.

II. Remember Whom You Represent.

Daniel was first and foremost a "servant of the living God" (Daniel 6:20). I'm not sure we understand the power of our representation of God.

A. We are *ambassadors* of Christ (2 Corinthians 5:20), which in the Greek is *presbuteros,* meaning "elder, overseer, one who is spiritually mature." An ambassador is directly commissioned by the emperor; responsible for bringing provinces into the kingdom; the ambassador is a stranger in a foreign land, who speaks on behalf of his native country and upholds the honor of his country. The ambassador (*presbuteros*) is . . .

1. One who is *mature*, having personal experience
2. One who is *responsible* not for his own word, but for the word of the one he serves and represents
3. One who is *commissioned* to bring hostiles into the kingdom
4. One who is *never ashamed to implore*, if necessary, because of the nobility of his calling
5. One who *represents* the name and authority of another.

B. We have been given authority to represent Christ (Matthew 28:18, 19; Luke 10:19; John 20:21-23). If we claim to be Christians, let us live up to the dignity of the name of Jesus and represent Him well. "Whoever claims to live in him must walk as Jesus did" (1 John 2:6).

Illustration

The story is told of Alexander the Great, who learned of a young commander in his army who lived in ways deemed unacceptable. His name, too, was Alexander. So he was summoned to appear before Alexander the Great, who told him, "Change your name or change your life."

III. Remember Why You Are Here.

We are to advance the kingdom of God on earth in all we do. Israel was called God's witness (Isaiah 43:10, 12). Jesus has commissioned us as His witnesses (Acts 1:8). We don't need to run and hide from the culture, but to invade it and to influence it as the salt of the earth. This was God's message to the exiles through the letter sent by Jeremiah (29:4-14).

In 1968, the country of Tanzania selected John Stephen Akwari to represent it in the Mexico City Olympics. Along the racecourse for the marathon, Akwari fell, severely injuring both his knee and ankle. By 7 p.m., a runner from Ethiopia had won the race, and all the other competitors had finished the race. Only a few thousand spectators were left in the vast stadium when a police siren at the gate caught their attention. Limping through the gate came number 36, Akwari, his leg wrapped in a bloody bandage. The onlookers began to cheer him on as he completed the final lap and crossed the finish line. Later, a reporter asked him, "Why did you continue the race after you were so badly injured and knew you had no chance of winning?" He replied, "My country did not send me 7,000 miles to start a race; they sent me to finish the race" (*Leadership*, "To Illustrate . . .").

Illustration

Launch Out Into the Deep

Text: Luke 5:1-11

I suppose if we all had one desire in common, it would be to be used of God for His glory. Sometimes that seems so out of reach. We feel as though we're not qualified. Or that we don't have enough Bible knowledge or spiritual maturity.

What kind of people does God use? If there was ever a person who was surprised that God not only called him into His service but did indeed use him in a powerful way, it was a first-century fisherman from Galilee known as Simon Peter.

Peter was introduced to Jesus by his brother, Andrew. When Jesus met him, He changed his name from Simon to Peter (John 1:40-42). Why the name change? *Simon* means "a reed." Here was a man blown by the winds of public opinion and shaken in his beliefs by the pressure of others. But Jesus saw something more in him, so He called him *Peter*, meaning "a rock"—one who would be strong and steadfast in his loyalty to Jesus and his commitment to the call of God.

His journey with Jesus was one of being transformed from a reed to a rock. His journey began one day with an encounter with Jesus by the Sea of Galilee. Peter had grown up and still lived in the town of Capernaum, located on the northern tip of the sea. The Sea of Galilee is about 13 miles long by 8 miles wide at 680 feet below sea level, giving it an almost tropical setting. During Jesus' time, there were nine townships around it with over 15,000 people.

Peter was in the fishing business with his brother, Andrew. They were partners with their close friends, James and John. On the day in question, these fishermen had just spent a tough night fishing, yet failed to catch anything. They were tired and frustrated. Around the shoreline, a crowd had gathered. The new controversial teacher, which some were saying was the Messiah, was preaching the Word of God. Simon listened from a distance.

Jesus had started His preaching in the synagogues. Synagogues were built in every Jewish town and city. Jews gathered each Sabbath for worship, prayer, the reading and exposition of the Scripture, and for fellowship. They also served as schools for the children during the week. One of Jesus' first sermons was delivered in the nearby town of Nazareth, where He had grown up (Luke 4:16-19).

But Jesus wasn't restricted to ministering in the synagogues. The world was His parish; the countryside, His sanctuary; every man's heart, His pulpit.

After addressing the crowd that day, Jesus noticed Simon and his companions, along with their boats on the shoreline. He asked to use Peter's boat so He could address the people offshore. After preaching, He turned to Peter and made an unusual request: "Launch out into the deep" (5:4, *NKJV*).

Did He merely mean the deep waters of Galilee? Not really. He was calling Simon into deeper waters with God. He was calling him to an adventure of faith with Him. He wanted to use Simon for His glory.

Jesus challenges you, "Launch out into the deep." There is more to life than fishing. There is more to life than the pleasures of this world. There is more to life than the pursuit of power, the achievement of fame, the accumulation of wealth. There is more to life than going through the daily routine—eating and drinking, sleeping and waking, working and resting, making money and preparing for retirement. There are deep waters in God that will fill your life with eternal purpose.

I. **God Uses Ordinary People.**

    A. *A fisherman, a common man* (Acts 4:13). This was one of the distinctive features of Jesus as a Rabbi. Traditionally, parents would save up enough money and then seek out a rabbi to teach their son whom they wanted to study the Law of God. Not so with Jesus. He sought out His followers, and He was no respecter of persons. To the Pharisees, He said, "The tax collectors and the prostitutes are entering the kingdom of God ahead of you" (Matthew 21:31).

    B. Here are three great lessons:

        1. Jesus initiates the search. God is searching for us (Luke 19:10).

        2. Jesus loves us just like we are.

        3. Jesus takes what we have and uses it for His glory.

    C. God uses FAT people—Faithful, Available, Teachable.

II. **God Uses Persevering People.**

    A. Perseverance is a greater resource than ability. Peter was tired. They had fished all night and had caught nothing. The effort failed, but he was willing to go back out and try again.

    B. The last couple of years I have had the opportunity to go fishing with a group of our men to Canada. If there's one thing I've learned about fishing, it is to cast your line one more time. Fishermen are a patient and persevering breed. A good fisherman always goes back into the same waters that discouraged him and tries again.

III. **God Uses Obedient People.**

    A. One of the greatest faith statements in the Bible is found in this beautiful passage: "Nevertheless at thy word I will let down the net" (Luke 5:5, KJV).

B. If there is one word you put in your vocabulary, put the
word *nevertheless*. It means "in spite of doubt, discouragement, disillusionment, failures of others, personal setbacks, personal failure, I will let down the net."

IV. God Uses Humble People.

A. *Humility* simply means "to recognize your need of God."
Look at Peter's honest heart: "Depart from me, for I am a
sinful man, O Lord!" (v. 8, *NKJV*).

B. *A mark of all God's servants.* Abraham said, "I am nothing
but dust and ashes" (Genesis 18:27). Jacob said, "I am less
than the least of all Your mercies" (see 32:10, *NKJV*). Job
said, "I repent and abhor myself" (see Job 42:6, *NKJV*).
Isaiah said, "Woe is me" (Isaiah 6:5). Paul said, "I am the
chief of sinners and the least of the apostles" (see 1 Timothy
1:15; 1 Corinthians 15:9). John Bradford, the faithful martyr for Christ, used to sign some of his letters with these
words: "A most miserable sinner, John Bradford."

C. Humility before God transforms us into servants to others.
We relinquish our desire to rule over others, to control, to
dominate, to intimidate, and to exercise authority. The disciples often got caught up in the quest for power. In Mark
9:33-35, Jesus said, "If anyone wants to be first, he must
be the very last, and the servant of all."

V. God Uses Visionary People.

A. Christ gives Peter a vision of what he can be and what he
can do for the kingdom of God: Do not be afraid; you will
catch men (Luke 5:10). From a reed to a vision of himself
as a rock.

B. Vision inspires loyalty. They left everything. I don't mean
they abandoned their families—they did not. These men
traveled with Jesus on ministry tours and then returned
home to raise their families (those who had them). They followed Him. The consummate word of discipleship is *follow*.

Norman Vincent Peale told the story of a friend who grew up very poor in a Midwestern city. His father told him he could only go through the lower grades, and then he would have to go to work to help support the family. One day he was walking down one of the main business streets of the city where he lived. He passed a newspaper office and saw a man sitting behind a desk with his coat off, vest unbuttoned, tie loose, sleeves rolled up, and the young boy was struck immediately as though transfixed. He asked the policeman at the corner, "Who is that man?"

"That man," replied the officer, "is the editor of that newspaper, and he is just about the most powerful influence in all this area."

"How did he get that job?" asked the boy.

"I don't know; he probably worked for it," the officer answered.

Right then the boy envisioned himself as the editor of that paper. The image was formed in his mind; he had no doubt about it at all. That was his future, and he went to work. At first he got a job delivering papers. Then he got on one of the trucks that took the papers out. Next, he moved into the advertising department and advanced rather rapidly. But this wasn't the normal path that led to the editorial chair.

The day came when the editor's position became open, and the publisher called him in and said, "Roger, I don't know why I'm going to make you this offer. You are the best advertising man we've ever had, but I have an overwhelming feeling that you were intended to be the editor of this paper. So I appoint you editor in chief."

"Thank you, sir," Roger said, "but God gave me the job years ago." The publisher listened in astonishment to Roger's story. He had a dream of what he could be, and it came to pass.

That day on the shoreline of Galilee, Peter caught a glimpse of the man he could be in Christ. And it came to pass.

The crux of the matter is this: They left everything and followed Him. How are you following Him today? Like Caleb (Numbers 14:24)? Peter at the Crucifixion (Luke 22:54)? The disciples (John 6:66)? David (Psalm 63:8)?

Christ calls and says, "Launch out into the deep."

Your Body, God's Temple

Text: 1 Corinthians 6:19, 20

The mystery of the human body reflects the majesty of God's creative work. We have . . .

- Eyes that can distinguish 8 million colors
- Ears consisting of 20,000 hairs discerning 300,000 tones
- A circulatory system that is 60-100 miles long
- A heart that pumps 5 quarts of blood per minute, 2,000 gallons per day; 1 billion red blood cells are produced every day; 200 miles of capillaries are developed for every pound of body fat.
- A muscle structure of 600 muscles that could lift 25 tons
- A nervous system consisting of 10 million nerves
- 1,300 nerve endings per square inch of fingertips that send touch sensations to the brain at the rate of 350 per second
- A skeletal structure consisting of 206 bones; 1 square inch of bone can withstand a 2-ton force.

- A digestive tract that is 30 feet long

- Lungs consisting of 600 million air sacs and breathe 2,400 gallons of air daily; the surface area of the lungs is 1,000 square feet, which is 20 times greater than the surface area of the skin.

- Skin—one square inch contains 19 million cells.

- 625 sweat glands, 65 hairs, 19 feet of blood vessels, 19,000 sensory cells, and 20 microscopic animals living on the skin's surface. The human skin is infested with mites; the body constantly sheds skin cells and replaces them with new ones; 75 percent of dust in the average house is made up of dead skin cells.

- A stomach that contains acid—one of the most powerful corrosives that can dissolve a razor blade; to keep from digesting itself, it produces a new lining every three days.

- A brain that weighs about 3 pounds and contains some 100 billion neurons—each neuron is like a small computer; more than 100,000 chemical reactions occur every second; nerve cells send impulses to the body at the rate of 200 mps; stores 10-15 trillion memories in a lifetime.

We hear all of that and identify with the psalmist when he declared, "I am fearfully and wonderfully made" (139:14). The most important truth about the human body is stated by Paul in 1 Corinthians 6:19, 20: "Your body is the temple of the Holy Spirit." Earlier he referred to the church corporate as the temple of God (3:16, 17). The word for *body* (*soma*) is singular. Furthermore, the word for *temple* (*naos*) refers to a sacred shrine, the sanctuary, not *hieron*, which refers to the entire area of a temple. The Holy of Holies is in view; the inner sanctuary of God.

The word *temple* or *tabernacle* or *sanctuary* means "the dwelling place of God." The concept of the temple occupies a central place in Scripture:

1. Moses' tabernacle (c. 1450 B.C.)
2. Solomon's temple (c. 950–586 B.C.)
3. Zerubbabel's temple (515 B.C.)

4. Herod's temple (20-19 B.C.)
5. Christ himself (John 2:19-21)
6. The church (Ephesians 2:21, 22)
7. The eternal temple (Revelation 21:1-3, 22)

I. **The Construction of the Temple**
Like the building of Moses' tabernacle and Solomon's temple, the Holy Spirit builds us spiritually into the kind of people God created us to be. Christians are people who are always "under construction." The church corporately is always being built by Christ (Matthew 16:18). Construction programs take longer and cost more than we think. So it is with personal spiritual growth and the process of building a congregation. The Christian life is progression, not perfection.

A man passed by the construction of a magnificent cathedral. As he passed a group of brick masons working on the project, he asked one of them, "What are you doing?" The man said, "I'm laying brick." So he asked another of the masons, "What are you doing?" He replied, "I'm constructing a wall." Finally, he asked a third brick mason, "What are you doing?" And he responded enthusiastically, "I'm building a cathedral!"

Illustration

II. **The Cleansing of the Temple (Matthew 21:10-17)**
A. The Temple Structure: Courts and the Temple Proper
1. The Court of Gentiles, into which any person could enter, but beyond which no Gentile could pass
2. The Court of Women, beyond which no woman could pass unless she was offering a sacrifice
3. The Court of the Israelites, where the offerings were given to the priests
4. The Court of the Priests, where the altar of burnt offering and the laver of cleansing stood
5. The Holy Place and the Holy of Holies, containing the ark of the covenant
B. Why Christ Cleansed the Temple
1. He acted as God's spokesman, claiming ownership of the Temple.

2. He functioned as the Judge who brings judgment first to His sanctuary (Ezekiel 9:6; 1 Peter 4:17).
3. He fulfilled the messianic expectation to restore the Temple and its glory. People had come from all over the world to the Temple to find God, yet they were met with extortion and materialism.
4. He condemned anything that hindered people's search for God.
5. He condemned the empty ritualism of the Temple service and called for heart obedience to God (Hosea 6:6; Matthew 9:13; 15:8).
C. The Cleansing Process of Our Lives
1. Self-cleansing (2 Corinthians 7:1)

Illustration

God Will See It. The story is told of a stonecutter in the Middle Ages who was working on a Gothic cathedral. He had spent days and weeks hewing out the features of a small figure to be placed on the top of the cathedral—not one of the prominent gargoyles that would sit atop the corners of the roof, but a smaller statue that would be tucked away in an obscure nook. Finally, an onlooker who had been watching these painstaking efforts, came up to him and said: "That's going to be a beautiful little statue, but tell me, why are you working so hard on it when you know that once it is up no one will see it?" The stonecutter replied, "God will see it."

2. God's cleansing (1 John 1:7-9). Only God can forgive and cleanse sin when we confess to Him and receive His forgiveness.

III. The Consecration of the Temple
To be consecrated means to be dedicated to the cause of Christ and to the will of God. There are three consecrations of the Temple in Scripture:
A. Moses and the Tabernacle (Exodus 40:34, 35)
B. Solomon and the Temple (2 Chronicles 5:14, 15)
C. Believers at Pentecost in the Temple court (Acts 2:1-4; 2 Corinthians 3:18)

Blessed in the Valley of Baca

Text: Psalm 84:5-7

O ne of the greatest books ever written is John Bunyan's *Pilgrim's Progress*. It aptly describes the Christian life as a journey. The psalmist uses this metaphor in verse 5 when he says believers have "set their hearts on pilgrimage." We are on a journey to a city with foundations whose builder and maker is God (see Hebrews 11:10).

On this pilgrimage we experience joys and sorrows; mountain peaks of victory and valleys of defeat; smooth, straight roads and rough, dangerous terrain. To put it frankly, the Christian pilgrimage is not always smooth sailing. This is one of the great misconceptions about faith—that we can take this journey without any difficulties. We try to sustain the euphoria of mountain-peak moments. Like the disciples on the Mount of Transfiguration, let's build three tabernacles and stay! People go from one religious meeting and revival service to the other, trying to keep the fire of emotionalism going.

The truth of the matter is, however, regardless of our person, position or possessions, we all pass through the "Valley of Baca" at one time or another. What is the Valley of Baca? The Hebrew word *Baca* means "weeping, sorrow, bitterness."

There are three valleys we experience on the pilgrimage of faith.

I. The Valley of Testing

    A. You can't have a testimony without a test. Look at those in the Bible who faced great tests:

        1. Abraham was tested by God (Genesis 22).

        2. Joseph was tested by imprisonment (39:20-23).

        3. Jesus was tested in the desert by the devil (Matthew 4:1-11).

        4. The early church was tested by persecution (Acts 5:41, 42; 8:1).

        5. Paul was tested in prison by Rome (see Acts 28; see also 2 Timothy 4:7, 8).

    B. We need to remember how God uses times of testing:

        1. To develop our character. God doesn't merely work around us, He works within us.

        2. In other words, God's not working on your situation, He's working on you! (see James 1:2-4).

II. The Valley of Tragedy

In a Gallup Poll taken several years ago, people were asked the following question: "If you met God face-to-face and asked Him one question, what would you ask?" The number one response was, "Why is there suffering in the world?" We've been asking the question since Adam and Eve sinned in Eden. The answer is really quite simple: When sin entered the world, death entered. The world is imperfect. In spite of technology, science and developments, the world remains imperfect, and none of us is exempt from the statistical probabilities of life. Jesus said, "These things I have spoken to you, that in Me you may have peace. In the world you will have tribulation; but be of good cheer, I have overcome the world" (John 16:33, *NKJV*). In the midst of evil, God is present to redeem and to save. Life may be bad, but God is good.

Illustration

Development of Braille. In the French Academy of Science there is a rather plain, old shoemaker's awl on display. The story behind the awl is quite extraordinary. To look at it, one would never suspect that this simple tool could be responsible for anything of consequence. In fact, it caused tremendous pain. This was the awl that one day fell from the shoemaker's table and put out the eye of the shoemaker's 9-year-old son. The injury was so severe that the boy lost vision in both eyes and was enrolled in a special school for children who were blind. The boy learned to read by handling large, carved-wood blocks. When the shoemaker's son became an adult, he thought of a new way to read. It involved learning a system of dots translated into the letters of the alphabet that could be read from a piece of paper on any flat surface. Louis Braille actually used the awl which had blinded him as a boy to form the dots into a whole new reading system for the blind—known today as Braille.

III. The Valley of Temptation

Temptation is a reality everyone faces, yet we can be victorious in Christ (1 Corinthians 10:13). As someone said, "I've had more trouble with myself than any other man I've ever met." How do we deal with failure and bounce back?

A. Failure comes in two forms:
   1. Moral failure: David (Psalm 51)
   2. Ministry failure: Peter (John 21)

B. Failure is not final (Micah 7:18; 1 John 1:9).

C. How do we maintain our motivation when we're in the valley? The psalmist gives us the key, "They make it a place of springs . . . they go from strength to strength" (84:6, 7).

Illustration

I heard the testimony of a Chinese pastor who was imprisoned for his faith. He was placed in solitary confinement because of his witness for Christ among the other prisoners. He won prisoners and guards to Christ. He was not allowed to have a Bible, to pray or to sing out loud. He was given a job working alone in the cesspool. As he entered the cesspool the first time and the door closed behind him, he was all alone. Suddenly he realized what a blessing he had. Since he was alone, and no one could hear him, he could pray and sing as loud and as long as he wanted. Month after month, he enjoyed deep fellowship alone with God in the cesspool. During his testimony, he said his favorite hymn was "In the Garden." During the interview I heard on the radio, he began to cite the first verse:

> I come to the garden alone,
> while the dew is still on the roses,
> And the voice I hear falling on my ear,
> the Son of God discloses.
> And He walks with me and He talks with me,
> and He tells me I am His own.
> And the joy we share as we tarry there,
> none other has ever known.

Then he said, "I survived those years alone in prison because I learned to turn a cesspool into a garden."

When Giving Thanks Is Tough

Thanksgiving Sermon

Text: 1 Thessalonians 5:16-18

One night the Biblical scholar Matthew Henry was robbed. When he got home he was still trembling with fear. Yet, he regained his calm as he prayed. This is the prayer he offered and wrote in his journal: "Father, I thank You first because I was never robbed before; second, I thank You because although they took my purse, they did not take my life; third, I thank You because although they took everything I had, it was not very much; and fourth, I thank You because it was I who was robbed and not I who robbed."

One of the greatest marks of spiritual maturity is the ability to give thanks when it's tough. This is what Paul meant in 1 Thessalonians 5:16-18: "Rejoice evermore. Pray without ceasing. In every thing give thanks: for this is the will of God in Christ Jesus concerning you" (KJV).

G.K. Chesterton, when asked what was the greatest lesson he had ever learned in life, said, "The greatest lesson I have learned is to take things with gratitude and not take them for granted." He also wrote, "You say grace before meals. All right. But I say grace before the concert and the opera, and grace before the play and pantomime, and grace before I open a book, and grace before sketching, painting, swimming, walking, playing, and grace before I dip the pen in the ink." Throughout the Scripture, we hear the call to give thanks. Thanksgiving is faith in action:

- Deuteronomy 8:10, 11: "When you have eaten and are satisfied, praise the Lord your God for the good land he has given you. Be careful that you do not forget the Lord your God."
- 1 Chronicles 16:8: "Give thanks to the Lord, call on his name; make known among the nations what he has done."
- Psalm 50:14: "Sacrifice thank offerings to God, fulfill your vows to the Most High."
- Psalm 107:22: "Let them sacrifice thank offerings and tell of his works with songs of joy."
- Colossians 1:12; 2:7; 3:15-17
- Ephesians 5:18-20
- Hebrews 12:28, 29; 13:15

Illustration

A woman had a parrot who always complained about everything. It was Thanksgiving Eve, and she was preparing the Thanksgiving meal. The parrot complained about everything as she worked. Finally, she had heard enough. She took him out of his cage and opened the refrigerator to put him in to punish him. "You'll stay in the refrigerator until you cool off and get control on your tongue," she said as she put him and closed the door. The parrot was stunned. Shivering, he caught a glimpse of the Thanksgiving turkey, skinned, legs pointing upward from the pan. The parrot said to the turkey, "Good heavens, man! What did you say?"

When you give thanks in tough times, thanksgiving does three things . . .

I. Cultivates Your Character

A. Notice that Paul says the cultivation of gratitude is the will of God. Cicero, the Roman poet, observed: "Thanksgiving is not only the greatest of all virtues, it is the parent of all virtues."

B. Parents recognize this principle when raising children. One of the first virtues we try to instill in them is the virtue of thanksgiving. Without it, they grow up to be selfish, narcissistic, manipulative, complaining, and thinking that the world owes them a living.

C. Focus on your "haves," not your "have-nots." The hymn says, "Count your blessings, name them one by one, and it will surprise you what the Lord has done." As the psalmist said, "Forget not all his benefits" (Psalm 103:2).

II. Increases Your Joy

A. Notice the connection between verses 16 and 18: *rejoicing* and *Thanksgiving*. It appears again in Colossians 1:12. The words *thanksgiving* and *joy* come from the same Greek root, *charis,* meaning "grace."

B. Thanksgiving is *eucharis,* and joy is *chara.* If you don't give thanks, what will you give? Anger, resentment, doubt, complaint? The secret to abounding joy is the gratitude attitude. I once read: "When you can't change the wind, adjust your sails."

"Be on the lookout for mercies. The more we look for them, the more of them we will see. Blessings brighten when we count them. Out of the determination of the heart, the eyes see. If you want to be gloomy, there's gloom enough to keep you glum; if you want to be happy, there's gleam enough to keep you glad. Better to lose count while naming your blessings than to lose your blessings by counting your troubles" (Maltbie B. Babcock, from *Inspiring Quotations*, compiled by Albert M. Wells Jr. and published by Thomas Nelson Publishers).

Illustration

III. Conquers Your Problems

A. I don't mean that all your problems go away when you give thanks. I mean that your problems stop being such a problem. You live from the inside out. What goes on around you no longer controls the condition of the world within you.

B. E. Stanley Jones said, "Bitterness comes to all. Sours some; sweetens others. I shall use it to sweeten my spirit."

You can't control the problems that come into your life—all the events that could be summed up in the phrase "In everything give thanks." But you can control how you respond.

C. Thanksgiving delivers us from a victim mentality and gives us a victor's mentality. I once read that nothing can help the person with the wrong mental attitude, and nothing can stop a person with the right mental attitude. And the right mental attitude to overcome your obstacles and win your battles is thanksgiving.

Do You Want to Get Well?

Text: John 5:1-15

The occasion was the Feast of Pentecost. The setting was the city of Jerusalem in the spring. There were three Jewish feasts of obligation—Passover, Pentecost and Tabernacles—which every male Jew within 15 miles of Jerusalem were required to attend. Furthermore, thousands of pilgrims made their journey to Jerusalem from all over the world for the great celebrations.

The place was the Pool of Bethesda in northeast Jerusalem. *Bethesda* means "house of mercy." The pool was surrounded by five covered porches. It was fed by underground springs and was deep enough to swim in. Great numbers of people suffering from various diseases gathered around the pool waiting for the water to be stirred by an angel. The first one to enter would be healed of his disease. Among the countless faces of those who were sick and suffering was a man who had been crippled for 38 years. Every day he joined numbers of others who waited for the healing waters of Bethesda to stir. Day after day, he went home disappointed. By now he was used to it.

During this particular feast, Jesus was in the northeast part of Jerusalem. He came to the great Pool of Bethesda. As He walked around the pool, He could not help but notice this man who had been crippled for 38 years. Why Christ went to him and not to others we will never know.

Almost nonchalantly Jesus approached the man and asked him a most unusual question: "Do you want to get well?" (v. 6). What a strange question to ask a crippled man. Yet, in the question we see the mission of the Messiah. Jesus came to make people well. Notice that Jesus did not ask him, "Do you want to be cured of your crippled condition?" Or, "Do you want to walk again?" His physical condition was only part of his problem. Jesus asked, "Do you want to get well?"

The word *well* (*hygies*) is the root of our English word *hygiene* and means "to make whole." The ministry of Jesus was not so much about healing as it was about wholeness. The word is used in Matthew 12:13; Mark 5:34; Acts 4:10; and Titus 2:8 to refer to "sound speech."

This is the meaning of salvation (*sozo*)—to make whole. Salvation is more than forgiveness for past sins; salvation is more than escape from judgment; salvation is more than deliverance from eternal separation. Jesus did not simply come into the world to save us from hell; He came to make us whole—spirit, mind and body. Christ came to restore humanity to the image of God.

Healing is . . .	*Wholeness is . . .*
temporary	eternal
instantaneous	progressive
remedial	developmental
partial	complete
external	internal

Holiness means "wholeness": "May God himself, the God of peace, sanctify you through and through. May your whole spirit, soul and body be kept blameless at the coming of our Lord Jesus Christ. The one who calls you is faithful and he will do it" (1 Thessalonians 5:23, 24).

Christ gives three steps to wholeness.

I.   Desire: "Do you want to get well?" (v. 6).

The first prerequisite to receiving the power of Jesus is to desire it. A.W. Tozer wrote about the pursuit of God. God will give you the desires of your heart (Psalm 37:3). Jesus awakened in the crippled man the hope that he could be healed and the desire to pursue the healing power of God. He enabled the man to see himself whole again. The first law of success in anything is desire. We have to want something bad enough before we get it. Look out for the three enemies of desire:

A.   *The loss of hope.* Perhaps he had lost hope of ever being well. He had watched others get healed, and yet he went home the same. He felt alone; no one to help.

B.   *The lack of responsibility.* Wellness requires responsibility for how we live in terms of diet, nutrition, exercise, rest, stress management, and so forth.

C.   *Complacency.* If we are content to stay as we are, there can be no change for us. We get caught living in a comfort zone, and that robs of the desire to want to change.

II. Determination: "Get up! Pick up your mat and walk" (v. 8).

A.   *Excuses.* At first the man offers an excuse: "I have no one to help me into the pool when the water is stirred." Then he adds, "While I am trying to get in, someone else goes down ahead of me" (v. 7). He feels powerless: "No one to help me." Although he admits that he has made some attempt to enter the water by himself: "While I am trying," he says.

B.   *Direction.* "Get up!" What a shocking imperative to make to a cripple. Yet, Jesus tells him to do the impossible. Be determined to do what you set your heart on doing. Do what you can do, and God will make up the difference.

1.   *Get up!* Don't stay where you are. Don't remain passive in the face of your affliction, setbacks, disappointments.

2.   *Pick up your mat.* The thing that had supported him, he would now carry. What an image to see this man carrying around his mat, the symbol of his helplessness.

He could accomplish the impossible. Do we realize our full potential? It is illustrated in God's estimation of the builders of Babel: "Nothing they plan to do will be impossible for them" (Genesis 11:6). This is what Paul meant in Philippians 4:13: "I can do all things through Christ" (*NKJV*).

3. *Walk.* The word is used in the present tense here and means "to walk and keep on walking." Wholeness is progressive. A change in lifestyle is in view.

C. *The spirit of determination in partnership with God.* As he got up, as he did what he could, Jesus made up the difference. This is what Pentecost is all about. Jesus left His disciples with an impossible task (Acts 1:8). How would it be possible that they could evangelize the world? Jesus made up the difference: "You will receive power."

III. Discipline: "Stop sinning or something worse may happen to you" (v. 14).

A. *Problem-solving or transformation?* Jesus did not simply come into this man's life to solve his physical problem. He came to transform his life. He later found him in the crowd and said, "Stop sinning." He called him to a life of repentance and faith. God's agenda is not to solve problems but to transform our lives. This is what wholeness is really all about—being like Jesus in every aspect of life (Romans 8:29).

B. *Failure to discipline.* To be truly whole we have to discipline our thoughts, feelings and behavior.
   1. *Cain* failed to discipline his anger, so he murdered his brother.
   2. *Esau* failed to discipline his appetite, so he sold his birthright.
   3. *Lot* failed to discipline the lust of his eyes, so he coveted the plains of Sodom and lost his family.
   4. *Samson* failed to discipline his strength, so he played games with God and forfeited his anointing.

5. *King Saul* failed to discipline his quest for power and lost his throne.

6. *David* failed to discipline his flesh, so he was unfaithful to God.

7. *Judas* failed to discipline the pursuit of self-interests, so he betrayed the Son of God with a kiss and died a suicide death.

8. *Pilate* failed to discipline his political aspirations, so he washed his hands of Jesus.

9. *The disciples* failed to discipline their fears, so they deserted Christ.

10. *Ananias and Sapphira* failed to discipline their love of money and lied to the Holy Spirit.

11. *Demas* failed to discipline his love for the world, so he left the ministry.

C. *Stop sinning!* There are three truths we need to know about sin:

1. Sin is destructive (Genesis 2:17).

2. Sin will be exposed (Numbers 32:23).

3. Sin can be cleansed (1 John 1:9). Where sin abounds, grace abounds much more (Romans 5:20). In Christ we can "put off [our] old self . . . put on the new self" (Ephesians 4:22-24).

Closing: What about you? Are you crippled by sin? Unforgiveness? Fear? Self-defeating thoughts? Ungodly behaviors and habits? Spiritual bondage? Bring your condition to Christ today for healing and take the steps of desire, determination and discipline to be well.

What to Do When You Feel Like Giving Up

Text: Luke 9:51-62

Henry Wadsworth Longfellow said, "Great is the art of beginning, but greater is the art of ending." Somewhere between beginning and ending we've all felt like giving up. Discouragement, disillusionment or disappointment set in, and we felt like saying, "I quit."

So, what do we do when we feel like giving up? In a word, God calls us to persevere. To *persevere* means "to persist in any purpose or endeavor; to continue striving for one's goals in spite of difficulties; to stay on course." The New Testament Greek word translated "perseverance" is *hupomone* and means both passive endurance and active persistence that presses on for the goal in spite of difficulties.

Perseverance makes the difference in life between success and failure. Perseverance is more important than talent, ability, aptitude and resources.

The Christian life demands perseverance. The gift of faith is free, but the life of faith is a fight. When asked to what level he attributed inspiration to the success of his work, William Faulkner, American author, replied: "Two percent inspiration, 98 percent perspiration." The Christians who suffered persecution in China used to have an affirmation: "Christians are like nails; the harder you hit us, the deeper we go."

One of the most important affirmations of faith is found in Philippians 3:14: "I press on toward the goal." The watchword of the hour is, *Press on!*

Press on, there's a . . .

- Heaven to be gained
- Reward to be received
- Dream to be fulfilled
- Finish line to be crossed
- Calling to be answered
- Enemy to be defeated
- Victory to be won
- Church to be built
- Harvest to be reaped
- World to be evangelized
- Kingdom to be established.

If anyone ever modeled perseverance, it was Jesus. His family questioned His validity. His disciples often doubted Him. The religious leaders by and large regarded Him as a fraud. Many followed Him only for His miracles and never accepted Him as Messiah. Sometimes I think we lose touch with His humanity. He was tempted as we are (Hebrews 4:15). He was rejected (John 1:10). Isaiah said that He was a man of sorrows and acquainted with grief (53:3). Yet, He persevered. In Luke 9:51-62, we see the great model of perseverance Jesus set for us to follow.

I.   Jesus Functioned out of His Will, Not His Emotions (v. 51).

   A. *Jesus resolutely set out for Jerusalem.* He "set [his] face like a flint" (see Isaiah 50:7). He was unmovable in His direction and purpose. Jerusalem meant arrest or even death. His disciples tried to discourage Him from taking this course. The fact that He functioned out of His will enabled Him to finish what He started. His last cry from the cross was, "It is finished" (John 19:30).

B. *The power of the human will.* Too often we are led by our emotions instead of our decisions. Emotions enrich our lives, but we cannot make the mistake of letting our emotions rule our lives. The issue is not what you *feel* but, rather, what you *will*. It's not what you feel but what you will that determines your success!

I'm sure . . .

- Noah didn't feel like building an ark—but in holy fear, he built an ark to save his family.
- Abraham didn't feel like taking Isaac to Moriah—but he arose early in the morning and set out to the place where God showed him. There he learned the meaning of *Jehovah Jireh*.
- Moses didn't feel like going to Egypt and confronting Pharaoh—but he went in obedience to God's command and saw the power of God displayed.
- Deborah didn't feel like leading Israel as a prophetess—but she took the challenge and led the nation to victory.
- David didn't feel like facing Goliath alone in battle—but he took his sling and five smooth stones and declared, "I come to you in the name of the Lord of hosts" (1 Samuel 17:45, *NKJV*).
- Jesus didn't feel like going to Calvary—but "for the joy set before Him, He endured the cross" (see Hebrews 12:2).
- Paul didn't feel like preaching at the cost of rejection, imprisonment and, eventually, a martyr's death—but he declared, "I have fought the good fight" (2 Timothy 4:7).

Illustration

When Olympic gymnast Kerri Strug was asked by her coach, Bela Karolyi, if she could do the vault that helped earn the U.S women a gold medal in team competition, she said, "Yes, I will, I will, I will."

Illustration

II. Jesus Was Proactive, Not Reactive to Life's Difficulties.

A. *He set out for Jerusalem.* In spite of the cost, He set out; He acted. Had He been a reactor, He would have retreated from the challenge. Let me ask you: What have you set out to be and to do in life? Are you still on course toward those goals, or have you been distracted?

B. *Take action in life.* Don't wait for life to happen. Go out there and make things happen!

Illustration

Mohammed Ali was once asked by a young man in college what he should do with his life. The heavyweight champion replied, "Stay in college, get the knowledge and stay there until you're through. If they can make penicillin out of moldy bread, they can sure make something out of you."

C. The four lepers teach us that victory comes through action, not passivity: "Why stay here until we die?" (see 2 Kings 7:3-11). God started working when they started walking. The victory doesn't come until we take the action we need to take to make things happen. Maybe it's time for you to stop waiting and start walking!

III. Jesus Weighed the Cost in Light of Heaven's Rewards (vv. 57-62).

The punch line: "No one who puts his hand to the plow and looks back is fit for service in the kingdom of God" (v. 62). Weigh the cost in light of rewards.

Three men that day offered Him three reasons why they couldn't follow Him. They thought the demands were too great, so they missed out on the opportunity of a lifetime to walk with Jesus.

When we devote our lives to Christ, we can know that there is an eternal reward waiting for us. There are five crowns in Scripture promised to us. The word *crown* speaks of the victor's wreath used in the Olympic Games, not a royal crown that belongs only to Jesus.

A. *Incorruptible crown* (1 Corinthians 9:25)
B. *Crown of righteousness* (2 Timothy 4:8)
C. *Crown of life* (James 1:12)
D. *Crown of glory* (1 Peter 5:4)
E. *Crown of reward* (Revelation 3:11)

Whatever cost you have to pay to be a disciple of Christ will be rewarded by God in this life a hundred times over and in the life to come with everlasting life!

Facing Your Failures

Text: John 21:1-17

D*id you know that...*

- Henry Ford failed to put a reverse gear in his first car?
- Thomas Edison failed in 2,000 experiments before he finally invented the lightbulb?
- The first time Benjamin Disraeli spoke before Parliament, members hissed him into silence and laughed when he said, "Though I sit down now, the time will come when you will hear of me"?
- Abraham Lincoln lost nine elections for political office and failed in business twice before finally being elected president?
- Albert Einstein was dismissed from school because he lacked interest in his studies, failed an entrance exam to a school in Zurich, and was later fired from his job as a tutor?
- Beethoven's music teacher, the brilliant John Albrechtsberger, said he would never compose any worthwhile music because he failed to follow the rules of musical composition?

- In 1932, when Fred Astaire was starting out, a Hollywood talent judge wrote on his screen test: "Can't act. Can't sing. Can dance a little"?
- Michael Jordan failed to make the junior-varsity basketball team when he tried out, and later the school principal told him to consider enlisting in the Air Force Academy after high school, which would be his best option for a career?

The road to success is lined with failures. Perhaps the fear of failure keeps more people from trying to reach their goals than any other factor.

Failure, like beauty, is in the eye of the beholder. For some, failure becomes their self-description. For others, it only becomes a fresh challenge pregnant with new opportunities. Some people want to play it safe. They just want security. No risks. But Douglas MacArthur said, "There is no security on this earth. There is only opportunity." It's interesting that the Chinese symbol for opportunity is also the symbol for crisis or danger. It's all in how you look at it.

The tragedy is that our desire for security and our fear of failure keeps us from ever attempting anything great in life and great for God. But nothing ventured, nothing gained. Until you are willing to risk, you will remain imprisoned in our world of fear.

- Faith is a risk.
- Love is a risk.
- Financial investing is a risk.
- Career change is a risk.
- Following your dream is a risk.
- Stealing home plate is a risk.
- Answering God's call to the ministry is a risk.
- Marriage is a risk.
- Having children is a risk.

But when you take the willingness to risk failure and couple it with sound wisdom and faith in God, nothing is impossible!

Sometimes failure hits us hard. Just like it did Simon Peter when he denied Christ. He went out from Caiaphas' "hall of judgment" and wept bitterly. But that's not enough. If all you do is weep bitterly over your failures, you will never be any better off for having failed. Don't waste your sorrows. Use your failures to become better, not bitter.

Here are five lessons we learn about facing our failures from Peter's experience.

I. Failure Is Never Final (v. 4).

A. *The seeking Shepherd.* After Jesus' resurrection, Peter still felt so discouraged and useless to God because he denied Jesus that he told the others, "I'm going fishing. Enough of this ministry business. I've failed. I'm going back to my comfort zone" (see v. 3). Then Jesus passed by, and that made all the difference. What a joy to know that Christ comes looking for us when we fail.

B. *"Early in the morning."* That says it all, doesn't it? The morning speaks of a new day, a new opportunity, a new beginning. We can put the past behind us and reach for what is ahead. It is not coincidence that the Resurrection took place in the morning. Luke 24:1, 2 says, "On the first day of the week, very early in the morning . . . they found the stone rolled away from the tomb." Perhaps that was the fulfillment of Malachi's vision of the Messiah, who said, "The Sun of righteousness shall arise with healing in His wings" (4:2, *NKJV*). Night may have set in your life, but the Sun of righteousness will shine on you because failure is never final.

II. Failure Does Not Change Our Status With God (v. 5).

A. *"Friends."* What a word of intimacy. He called them friends the night of the Last Supper (John 15:15). Let me remind you of two vital aspects of Christ's friendship, which, by the way, does not bring God down to our level nor us up to His. It does mean that we are close to Him, and He is close to us. Even Abraham was called the friend of God (2 Chronicles 20:7), and Moses spoke with Him as His friend (Exodus 33:11). By the way, have you seen the new bumper sticker, "Friends don't give friends fruitcakes"?

B. *The Prodigal Son: servant or son?* After the Prodigal Son comes to his senses and realizes what a colossal mess he's made of his life, he says to himself, "I will set out and go back to my father and say to him: 'Father, I have sinned against heaven and against you. I am no longer worthy to be called your son; make me like one of your hired men'" (Luke 15:18, 19). Why does he make such a statement? Because he cannot fathom a forgiveness great enough to restore his relationship with his father like it was before he left. As far as he was concerned, his youthful rebellion and indulgent lifestyle, which had cost him his inheritance and left him penniless, was enough to permanently ruin their relationship. Now for the rest of the story:

> So he got up and went to his father. But while he was still a long way off, his father saw him and was filled with compassion for him; he ran to his son, threw his arms around him and kissed him. The son said to him, "Father, I have sinned against heaven and against you. I am no longer worthy to be called your son." But the father said to his servants, "Quick! Bring the best robe and put it on him. Put a ring on his finger and sandals on his feet. Bring the fattened calf and kill it. Let's have a feast and celebrate. For this son of mine was dead and is alive again; he was lost and is found" (vv. 20-24).

Do you get the picture? The Prodigal refers to himself as a servant. But his father calls him "my son." There's a world of difference between a servant and a son. The point is, the father's forgiveness had fully restored their relationship as if it had never been severed.

III. Failure Can Be Transformed Into Success (v. 6).

A. *"Throw your nets in again."* Try again. I can still recall my father telling me the story of the little train ascending the steep side of the mountain: "I think I can . . . . I knew I could . . . ." The point is, try again. There is no shame in trying and failing. The shame lies in being too afraid to try in the first place. They caught 153 fish. Some early-church leaders said this referred to the 153 different kinds of fish in the sea identified by the famous Greek fishermen, referring to their success to evangelize the entire world.

B. *Try again!*

Illustration

After being expelled from college, Duke Rudman drifted into jobs in Texas oil fields. As he gained experience, he dreamed of independent oil exploration. Whenever he would get a few thousand dollars together, he leased drilling equipment and sank a well. He drilled 29 wells in two years and came up dry every time. Nearing the age of 40, he remained unsuccessful. He began studying land formations, shale types, and other aspects of geology to improve his chances. He leased his 30th tract of land, and this time a huge oil reservoir was discovered. Three out of every four holes he drills is dry. After 60 years, he says he believes he has failed more than anyone in the business, but he has struck oil enough times to earn millions of dollars. "There were days I wanted to quit," says Rudman, "but I'd just push the thought away and get back to work."

IV. Failure Does Not Mean You Are a Failure (v. 12).

A. *"Come and have breakfast."* The communal meal of close friendship is depicted so beautifully. Now this ought to be a scene with which we can all identify. I mean, Christians eat as well as anyone. Eating is synonymous with fellowship. The bread and the fish reminded them of the feeding of the 5,000; the Passover; the two disciples on the Emmaus Road when their eyes were opened.

B. *Failure does not permanently scar your life.* We must be careful about generalizing failure until we become one with our failures. True, sin leaves scars—dome worse than others. It does take time to heal and to be restored. But, in Christ, old things pass away, and all things become new! Jesus' invitation is, "Come and have breakfast!"

V. Failure Does Not Disqualify Us for Kingdom Service (vv. 15-17).

    A. Jesus told Peter, "Feed my sheep." Here's the point: Jesus was giving him a second call to his ministry, just like He had given to him nearly four years earlier at that same spot on the Galilee when He said, "Come, follow me" (Matthew 4:19; Mark 1:17).

    B. God is the God of a second chance. We see this same principle in Jonah's life: "The word of the Lord came to Jonah a *second time*" (3:1); and also in Jeremiah's life, when God spoke to him a second time (33:1).

Closing: Whatever failure you have experienced, get back up today by grace, and get back in the game of life and in your calling to ministry because God's not finished with you yet!

The Spirit Makes the Difference

Pentecost Sunday Sermon

Text: Acts 2:38, 39

There is no way to talk about the Christian life without talking about the person and work of the Holy Spirit. The Holy Spirit is mentioned 261 times in the New Testament alone. The Holy Spirit makes the difference. Your spiritual growth and maturity is directly proportionate to your submission to the work of the Holy Spirit in your life. When we talk about the Holy Spirit, we are not talking about a New Age mysticism, cosmic power, emotionalism or psychic phenomenon. He is God, third member of the triune Godhead; coexistent, eternal, and equal with the Father and Son (Matthew 28:19). Jesus described Him in very personal terms in John 14:16, 17.

When we read the Book of Acts, it becomes apparent that the coming of the Holy Spirit on the Day of Pentecost marked a dramatic transformation in the lives of the disciples and, in particular, Simon Peter. Before Pentecost, Peter was often impulsive in his decisions, fearful of opposition and unstable in his commitments. But after Pentecost, he emerges on the scene as a courageous, committed and faithful disciple of the Lord Jesus Christ. Peter's challenge rings clear

today: "You will receive the gift of the Holy Spirit" (Acts 2:38).
What is this gift, and how do we receive it?

I.   Receiving the Spirit at Conversion

We have the Holy Spirit the moment we receive Christ as our
Savior. He lives in the heart of every believer, making us the
temple of God (1 Corinthians 6:19, 20). The Spirit is at work in
every believer's life (John 20:22).

- Born-again by the Spirit (John 3:3-7)
- Led by the Spirit (Romans 8:14)
- Intercedes for us in prayer (vv. 26, 27)
- Seals us for the day of salvation (Ephesians 1:13)
- Guides us into all truth (John 16:13)
- Gifts us for service (1 Corinthians 12:11)
- Transforms us into Christ's image (2 Corinthians 3:18)

II. Receiving the Spirit in His Baptism or Infilling

Every believer needs to receive the baptism in the Holy Spirit,
or what is also described in Scripture as being filled with the
Holy Spirit, for power.

A. *There are five accounts in Acts of believers being filled
   with the Spirit:*
   1. Pentecost (2:4)
   2. Samaria (8:14-17)
   3. Paul (9:17)
   4. Cornelius (10:44-46)
   5. Ephesus (19:6)

B. *The purpose of the infilling:* One word, *power* (1:8). The
   word in Greek is *dynamis*, from which we get the word
   dynamite!
   1. Power from on high (Luke 24:49)
   2. Power in the inner man (Ephesians 3:16, 17).
   3. Power in weakness (2 Corinthians 12:9)

III. Receiving the Spirit in Seasons of Renewal

There are seasons of spiritual renewal and new power as we

seek God to fill us again with the Spirit as seen in the life of the early church (Acts 4:31; 13:52; Ephesians 5:18).

Closing: How can we be filled with the Spirit? Peter tells us to "receive." The word *receive* tells us first and foremost what we do not have to do: work, labor, tarry, be perfect. This means we receive the Spirit as we would receive a gift (Acts 2:38) or as we would receive a guest. The KJV translates *Holy Spirit* as "Holy Ghost," from the Anglo-Saxon derivative, *guest*. Thus, the translators in 1611 meant *Divine Guest.* The means of receptivity include:

- Desiring the gift (Matthew 5:6)
- Asking for the gift (Luke 11:13)
- Repenting of any sins and barriers between you and God's will in your life (Acts 2:38).

Missionary Hudson Taylor said, "The Holy Spirit only enters the human heart that can boast of nothing but an aching void."

When Revival Comes

Text: Revelation 2:1-7

Revival . . . we hear the word a lot these days. What is revival? The word *revival* simply means "a coming back to life again." It describes a spiritual awakening; a restoration of spiritual passion; a renewal of faith; a returning to God. A revival is more than emotionalism or spiritual phenomena.

One of the biggest misconceptions about revival is that revival is only needed by those who have fallen away from God—for those who are "backslidden," to use an old-fashioned term. The truth is that revival is needed in every believer's life, in every church's life. We all need seasons of spiritual renewal where the latter rain of the Holy Spirit is poured out to refresh and renew us. So, our prayer for revival is not an indictment but, rather, a recognition of our need of God. In other words, good churches need revival too.

Revival is both personal and corporate. Throughout the Scripture, we hear a stream of prayers for revival:

- Psalm 51:10-13: "Create in me . . . restore to me the joy of your salvation and grant me a willing spirit, to sustain me. Then will I teach transgressors . . ."

- Psalm 85:6: "Will you not revive us again, that your people may rejoice in you?"
- Isaiah 44:3: "For I will pour water on the thirsty land, and streams on the dry ground; I will pour out my Spirit on your offspring, and my blessing on your descendants."
- Joel 2:28, 29
- Acts 3:19

What is a revival? It was a revival when . . .

- Samuel interceded at Mizpah (1 Samuel 7:2-6)
- Elijah prevailed at Carmel (1 Kings 18:39)
- Hezekiah called the nation to repentance (2 Chronicles 30:18-20)
- Ezra proclaimed the Word (Nehemiah 8:10)
- John the Baptist announced the Messiah (John 1:29)
- Jesus ushered in the kingdom of God (Matthew 4:17)
- The Spirit came at Pentecost (Acts 2:4)
- The martyred church stood firm under the persecution of Rome.

The Reformation was born under men like John Wycliffe, Martin Luther and John Calvin. The first Great Awakening came in the 1700s with John and Charles Wesley in England. The Puritans and Anglicans founded Harvard and Yale to educate ministers. Jonathan Edwards (c. 1750) led a revival in Massachusetts. George Whitefield, associate of the Wesleys, began preaching tours in the U.S. David Brainerd and others preached to the American Indians and African-Americans.

The second Great Awakening came in the 1800s. The Sunday school outreach began in England. World mission endeavors were birthed through William Carey and David Livingstone. Inner-city revivals emerged with D.L. Moody. The church acted to abolish slavery and to secure women's rights. Charles Finney's revival in New York (1824) produced far-reaching results.

Revival came in the early 1900s with . . .

- The Asuza Street Revival

- Billy Graham's evangelistic crusades in the 1950s where he preached Christ to the world
- The Charismatic Renewal broke through denominational barriers
- Dr. Martin Luther King Jr. led the Civil Rights Movement and brought social justice.
- The modern church growth movement and the seeker-sensitive movement opened the door of the Kingdom in new and dynamic ways to the lost of this generation.

Past revivals are great, but we, too, need revival. Our hearts are hungry. Our prayers are ascending heavenward. We are not content to live on yesterday's manna. We cry out with the psalmist, "Will you not revive us again, that your people may rejoice in you?" (85:6).

We learn important truths about revival from Jesus' message to the Ephesian church in Revelation 2:1-7. This church was founded by Paul on his second missionary journey. He preached there for two years, and from Ephesus, the message of Christ was preached in the entire area so that everyone heard the word of the Lord.

On the one hand, Ephesus was a great church. Christ commended them for their *service* (deeds, hard work, perseverance); their *stance* (they did not tolerate wicked men, they tested those who claimed to be apostles and were not, and found them to be false, they hated the practices of the Nicolaitans); and their *steadfastness* (they endured hardships for His name and did not grow weary). Yet, they needed revival. What are the conditions and marks of real revival? When revival comes, there is . . .

I.   A Rekindling of Our Love for God

A. "You have left your first love" (Revelation 2:4, *NKJV*). You have abandoned, or forsaken, your first love. What is "first love"? The analogy is made to the inception of love, a deep passion for God, a pure love for Jesus unencumbered by the weights of human religion, uncomplicated with the details of theological doctrine. Wilson Carlisle, founder of the Christian Army said, "Jesus captured my heart. For me to know Jesus is a love affair."

B.   The greatest mark of revival is a rekindling of our love for God (Deuteronomy 6:5).

II. A Refreshing of the Spirit's Power

A.   "Remember the height from which you have fallen" (Revelation 2:5). What does He mean? I believe He is recalling their remembrance to their beginning point—the outpouring of the Spirit (Acts 19:1-6). The Ephesian church was born out of a reenactment of Pentecost. E. Stanley Jones said in *The Way to Power and Poise,* "The Holy Spirit has been lost in large measure from modern Christianity. We are presenting a Holy Spiritless Christianity—a demand without a dynamic."

B.   Pentecost is a recurring experience in the believer's life (Acts 1:8; 4:31; 13:52). In Ezekiel's vision of the valley of the dry bones (Ezekiel 37:1-10), when he prophesied to the wind (that is, the Holy Spirit), they stood on their feet as an exceedingly vast army. When the Spirit blows the wind of Pentecost in the church, we, too, stand up as an exceedingly vast army, and the gates of hell shall not prevail against us!

III. A Return to the Basics

A.   "Repent and do the things you did at first" (Revelation 2:5). Return to the basics of discipleship and the essential ministry of the church. The German adage is apropos; "The main business is to keep the main business the main business."

B.   The church often gets distracted from its mission. One church analyst observes that 70 percent of America's churches are in a survival mode; 25 percent are in a success mode; and only 5 percent, in his opinion, have moved past success to dealing with issues of significance (David Shibley, "What Is God Saying to the American Church?" *Global Advance Update* [Summer/Fall 1996]).

In an article in the *Atlantic Monthly*, Peter Drucker says: "Every agency, every policy, every program, every activity, should be confronted with these questions: What is your mission? Is it still the right mission? Is it still worth doing? If we were not doing this, would we go into it now?" These questions get at the heart of honest self-evaluation, enabling any organization, whether spiritual or secular, to remain on the cutting edge.

Illustration

These are the questions we need to ask ourselves today as the church of Jesus Christ and return to our mission of making disciples of all nations (Matthew 28:19). If we succeed at this simple mission, we will hear Christ say to us, "Well done, good and faithful servants" (see Matthew 25:21, 23).

Unfading Beauty

Mother's Day Sermon

Text: 1 Peter 3:1-7

It has been said that beauty is only skin-deep. That depends on how you define *beauty*. Beauty is subjective. Beauty is in the eye of the beholder. Webster defines *beauty* as "the quality of objects, sounds, ideas, attitudes, and so forth, that pleases and gratifies as by their harmony, pattern, excellence, or truth." Beauty arouses aesthetic pleasure.

Our culture puts a high premium on beauty. Beauty is power. Magazines publish endless lists of the world's most beautiful people. Women of all ages today feel relentless pressure to be as beautiful as they can. Unfortunately, beauty is often defined by standards set by Hollywood and the fashion industry.

But what is true beauty in the eyes of God? Proverbs 31:30 gives the most important definition of beauty for women: "Charm is deceptive, and beauty is fleeting; but a woman who fears the Lord is to be praised." The greatest beauty a woman can have is spiritual beauty.

A woman parked her brand-new Lexus in front of her office, ready to show it off to her colleagues. As she got out, a truck passed too close and completely tore off the door on the driver's side. The woman immediately grabbed her cell phone, dialed 911, and within

Illustration

minutes, a policeman pulled up. Before the officer had a chance to ask any questions, the woman started screaming hysterically. Her Lexus, which she had just picked up the day before, was now completely ruined and would never be the same, no matter what the body shop did to it. When the woman finally wound down from her ranting and raving, the officer shook his head in disgust and disbelief. "I can't believe how materialistic you women are. You are so focused on your possessions that you don't notice anything else."

"How can you say such a thing?" asked the woman. The cop replied, "Don't you know that your left arm is missing from the elbow down? It must have been torn off when the truck hit you." "Oh my goodness!" screamed the woman. "Where's my tennis bracelet?"

I.   The Beauty of Outward Behavior (vv. 1-2, 7)

- "Wives, in the same way be submissive to your husbands so that, if any of them do not believe the word, they may be won over without words by the behavior of their wives" (v. 1).
- "When they see the purity and reverence of your lives" (v. 2).
- "Husbands, in the same way be considerate as you live with your wives, and treat them with respect as the weaker partner and as heirs with you of the gracious gift of life, so that nothing will hinder your prayers" (v. 7).

Peter is concerned for Christian women who are married to men without Christ. He says they "do not believe the word" (Logos, Jesus, the Word—John 1:1, 14). Actually, it means they have heard the gospel, but they have deliberately set themselves against the truth. Their wives have preached to them, as they should, and are now to wait on God in prayer and trust the Holy Spirit to do the work. They can win them over without words by the power of their behavior. Now words are important, but lifestyle is more important. *When they see your behavior* means to see for oneself, to watch attentively.

   A. *Submission.* It means to support and to hold up. It means to show proper respect. Submission is for everyone, not just wives: Submission begins with God (James 4:7);

husbands are to treat their wives as equal partners (1 Peter
3:7); marriage is mutual submission (Ephesians 5:21);
children are commanded to submit (6:1-3); Christ modeled
submission (1 Peter 2:21-24). Peter begins chapter 3 with,
"In the same way," referring to the submission of Christ.

B. *Purity and reverence.* Purity of life comes from reverence
for God.

Augustine writes in *Confessions* how his mother, Monica,
prayed for both him and his father, who was saved only shortly
before he died. He records her love and patience toward them in
their spiritual rebellion. Yet, he became one of the most influential
Christian leaders in the history of the church.

Illustration

II. The Beauty of Inward Character (vv. 3, 4)

"Your beauty should not come from outward adornment, such
as braided hair and the wearing of gold jewelry and fine
clothes. Instead, it should be that of your inner self, the unfading beauty of a gentle and quiet spirit, which is of great worth
in God's sight."

A. *Outward adornment.* Roman women adorned themselves
so extravagantly that they stacked their hair high on their
heads and covered themselves with jewels. The word *wearing* in Greek means "to wrap jewels all over the body." This
is not a prohibition on fashion or jewelry, but it is an emphasis on cultivating real beauty within. God does not look at
the outward appearance, but He looks on the heart (1
Samuel 16:7). The word *appearance* is *kosmos,* for "order-
ly" as opposed to chaos. Outward adornment should corre-
late with the real person, not masquerade. There should be
cosmos, not chaos, between who we are on the inside and
how we present ourselves on the outside.

B. *Inward character.* The inner self is more important that
outward beauty, temporary wealth and fame. The *inner
self* actually reads in Greek, "the hidden man or person of

the heart." The heart is the essence of our personality, that part of us that makes us able to commune with God. It's easy to get caught up in the materialism of our day. *Unfading* means free from decay and theft (see Matthew 6:19-21; 1 Peter 1:23). Two qualities are called for: *gentleness*, which is great power under great control (see Matthew 11:28-30; 2 Corinthians 10:1); and *quietness* (Greek, *hesuchios*), which means "peaceable; tranquil; causing no disturbance to others; to be still; and to hold your peace." This does not mean to remain silent on important issues. But it does mean to show restraint.

C. James Dobson points out that the average man speaks about 25,000 words a day, while the average woman speaks about 50,000 words. What happens is that when a husband gets home in the evening, he has used up 24,999 and grunts his way through the evening, but she has another 25,000 words to go!

III. The Beauty of Upward Faith (vv. 5, 6)

Godly women put their hope in God and do not give way to fear. They need to model faith, not fear, in their families. Sarah was a woman of faith. She and Abraham accepted the call to leave their home (Genesis 12), to believe for a miracle child (ch.18) and to offer Isaac to God (ch. 22).

Illustration

Dr. Marianne Neifert said, "If I hadn't had children, I probably would have had more money and material things. I probably would have gone more places, gotten more sleep, pampered myself more. My life would have been much more boring and predictable. As a result of being a parent, I have laughed harder, cried more often. I have worried more and hurried more. I've had less sleep, but somehow I've had more fun. I've learned more, grown more. My heart has ached harder, and I've loved to a capacity beyond my imagination. I've given more of myself, but I've derived more meaning from life" (from a speech, quoted in *Reader's Digest*).

Unfailing Love. I heard the testimony of a mother struggling with her rebellious daughter. The rebellion started right after her parents were divorced. It all culminated the night the police called the mother to pick up her daughter, who had been arrested for DUI, at the police station. They didn't speak until the next morning. The mother went into her daughter's room and broke the silence by giving her a small, gift-wrapped box. Her daughter nonchalantly opened it and found a small piece of rock. She rolled her eyes and said, "Cute, Mom. What's this for?" Her mother said, "Here's the card." The daughter opened the card, read it and dropped it to the floor, then hugged her mother as they wept together. Written in the card were these words: "This rock is more than 200 million years old. That's how long it will take before I give up on you" (Bob Gilbert and Karen Wydra, *Bits and Pieces,* July 16, 1998, pp. 16-17).

Illustration

Running From God

Text: Jonah 1:1-17

The history of humanity is the story of man running from God. When God created us, He endowed us with a unique power—the power of choice. Adam and Eve chose to disobey God. In essence, they were running away from God's will, purpose and command. A teenager told me he wished we could find the Garden of Eden. I asked why. We would only ruin it again.

There are times when we run from God. Such is the case of Jonah. We don't know much about Jonah except that he was from Galilee in northern Israel. God called him to go to Nineveh and preach against it, but he ran away from the Lord. Three times in the first chapter of Jonah we read that he ran away from the Lord.

What was going on to make him run away?

The city of Nineveh was built originally by Nimrod (Genesis 10:8-11). By Jonah's time, it was the capital of Assyria with a population of 120,000—second in size only to Babylon. It was located about 550 miles northeast of Samaria, the capital of Israel. It would have taken Jonah about a month to make the journey. Assyria was a violent empire. Four Assyrian kings are mentioned in the Old Testament who invaded Israel. Jonah ministered between 800 and 750 B.C. Later, in 722 B.C., Assyria invaded Israel and dispersed the people. Yet, God cared about the Assyrians. In spite of the wickedness of the people, God called an Israeli prophet to go and preach the word of the Lord for their salvation.

God's challenge to Jonah was to go to the archenemy of Israel and tell them of God's love and grace; to warn them of the judgment to come and call them to repentance. But Jonah didn't want the people of Nineveh to repent. He wanted God to judge them for their wickedness and harsh treatment of Israel, so he ran away from the Lord.

I. Why Did Jonah Run From God?

There were several attitudes in Jonah that caused him to run from the call of God.

A. *Exclusivity.* He wanted God to bless Israel but not Nineveh. He desired mercy for his own people and judgment for others. He was unwilling to confront his attitudes, so he ran from God.

B. *Comfort zone.* He refused to take the risk of faith. Life was good; he had a comfortable lifestyle, everyone accepted his ministry, and Israel enjoyed a time of prosperity and peace. Why upset the applecart? So he ran from God.

C. *Rebellion.* He claimed ownership of his own life and ministry. He was told to do something he didn't want to do, so he ran from God.

D. *Anger at God.* He did not like God's plan to save the people of Nineveh. God should judge them, he thought, so he ran from God.

E. *Fear.* He feared the consequences. After all, what might happen to him if he approached Israel's archenemy and demanded them to repent? It might mean his life.

F. Are you running from God today? Are you running from . . .

1. *God's call to salvation?* I talked with a young man for over an hour about the salvation of Jesus Christ. I said

"I would love to pray with you now, to lead you in the sinner's prayer," but he said, "No. I need to think about it more."

2. *God's call to sanctification*? Is there an area of your life that God has convicted? Has He called you to surrender that sin, problem, attitude to Him, but you've held on to it? Are you like the Prodigal Son living in the far country? Are you like Adam and Eve hiding from God in the garden because of the guilt of your sin?

3. *God's call to service*? Has He called you to an area of ministry . . . the mission field . . . a ministry in the church . . . but you've resisted?

II. The Pursuit of God

Although Jonah ran from God, God ran after him. The good news of the gospel is that God always comes looking for us. How did God pursue Jonah?

A. *The violent storm* (vv. 1-5). "The Lord sent a great wind on the sea, and such a violent storm arose that the ship threatened to break up" (v. 4). God will not leave us in our rebellion. He will still send a violent wind in our lives to break up our fallow ground and bring us to repentance. It is interesting that this same wind came on the Day of Pentecost as a sign of the Holy Spirit. The Spirit blows as a violent wind in our lives when we run from God.

B. *The confrontation of others* (vv. 6-12). Jonah was sleeping. This is a type of spiritual drowsiness. The captain and crew confront him. Their questions are the questions of the Holy Spirit to us when we run from God:

1. "What do you do?" or, "What are you doing on this ship?"
2. "Where do you come from?"
3. "What is your country?"
4. "From what people are you?"
5. "What have you done?"

a. They reawaken in him his sense of identity and calling. He says, "I am a Hebrew and I worship the Lord, the God of heaven, who made the sea and the land" (v. 9). When we run from God, He convicts us to bring us back to making the declaration:
   (1.) I am a person of the covenant.
   (2.) I am a worshiper of God.
   (3.) I am a minister of the gospel of Christ.
b. Regardless of who you are or what you've done, God has not given up on you. God is looking for you, calling you to Himself so that His will might be fulfilled in your life. Nothing can separate you from the love of Christ (Romans 8:39).

C. *The response to God's call* (v. 12). The crucial question asked is, "What should we do?" (v. 11). He says, "Pick me up and throw me into the sea" (v. 12). They tried everything else but to no avail. Finally, they threw him into the fierce waters of the Mediterranean, and the sea grew calm. Before Jonah drowned, the Lord provided a great fish that swallowed him.

III. The Lessons Learned

It's an inspiring Bible story, but what does it mean to us?

A. *God uses imperfect vessels.* Jonah was anything but perfect. Yet, God called him and commissioned him. Many believers struggle with feeling unworthy of God's grace and calling. To say that God uses imperfect vessels is not to condone open sin and rebellion. When the people of Nineveh saw an Israeli prophet in their midst, they realized it had to be God at work, because he would have never gone there of his own accord.

B. *Favorable circumstances do not always indicate the blessings of God.* When he went to Joppa, he found a ship bound for the port of Tarshish. He could have told himself God was providing the ship. We have the tendency to deceive ourselves when we want something too much.

C. *When we run from God, God pursues us.* Jonah came to terms with the inescapable God that David describes in Psalm 139:1-10.

D. *God requires total surrender.* Jonah's request, "Throw me into the sea," was, in effect, him saying, "Put me in the hands of God." He did not know God would sent a great whale to deliver him. The principle of surrender is seen here. Jonah had to die to his own will, his prejudices and his rebellion.

D.L. Moody heard the testimony of a businessman that changed the course of his life: "The world has yet to see what God can do in and for and through and with a man totally yielded in his heart." As a young man, Dwight Moody prayed in his heart, "God, I want to be that man."

Illustration

Here Comes That Dreamer!

Text: Genesis 37:1-11, 19, 20

I t has been said that a man is never old until regrets take the place of his dreams. Martin Luther King Jr. rallied the Civil Rights Movement behind one clarion call: "I have a dream!"

We use the word *dream* in a variety of ways. When we think of dreams, we usually think of dreams in the night. But dreams are also visions, goals and aspirations.

What is your dream? What do you envision for your life? What do you hope for or long for? What are your goals and aspirations? Our dreams determine the quality of our lives. Proverbs 23:7 says, "As he thinks in his heart, so is he" (*NKJV*). Without a dream for our lives, we drift aimlessly through life, reacting to one circumstance after another. Without a dream, we lack the master plan by which to build our lives. Proverbs 29:18 reminds us, "Where there is no vision, the people perish" (KJV).

On the other hand, when we possess a dream for our lives inspired by God, then we live with a plan. Each day, every decision fits into a larger plan as our dreams become reality. God gives dreams and visions for life (Joel 2:28, 29; Hosea 12:10; Acts 26:19). One of the best-loved personalities in the Bible is Joseph. As children we remember hearing about his beautiful coat of many colors. We know him as a man with a dream from God that shaped his destiny.

Here's a synopsis of what happened: He was 17 years old and the favorite son of Jacob, who had 12 sons. He brought a bad report about his brothers to his father. He had two dreams during the night. In dream #1 he saw sheaves of grain. His sheaf rose up, and their sheaves bowed down to his. In dream #2 the sun, moon and 11 stars were bowing down to him. When he shared his dreams with his family, they resented him, and his father rebuked him. Eventually, his other brothers, excluding Benjamin, the youngest, sold Joseph into slavery to a wandering band of Ishmaelites who took him to Egypt and sold him to Potiphar. But in Egypt his dream became reality.

I.   Joseph Dreamed When He Was Young (37:2).

    A. *The importance of youth* (Ecclesiastes 12:1; 1 Timothy 4:12). Most people accept Christ as their Savior before they reach age 18, and most people who accept the call of God to full-time ministry do so before they are 21.

    B. These people dreamed while young:

        1. Pascal wrote a great work at 16 and died at only 37.

        2. Raphael painted his works at a very young age and died at 37.

        3. Alfred Tennyson wrote his first volume at 18.

        4. Victor Hugo wrote a tragedy at age 15, at 17 received prizes at a poetry competition and earned the title "master" before he was 20.

        5. John Calvin joined the Reformation at 21 and at 27 wrote *The Institutes of the Christian Religion.*

        6. Isaac Newton was 24 when he formulated the law of gravity and made some of his greatest discoveries before he was 25.

        7. Charles Dickens wrote *Pickwick Papers* at 24 and *Oliver Twist* at 25.

8. Charles Spurgeon was a powerful preacher in his early 20s, and by 25 he pastored the largest church in London.

9. Jonathan Edwards made five resolutions in his youth, which guided him throughout his life: "To live with all my life while I do live; to never lose one moment of time, but to improve it in the most profitable way I possibly can; never to do anything that I should despise or think meanly of in another; never to do anything out of revenge; and never to do anything which I should be afraid to do if it were the last hour of my life."

C. Dreams are also for those who are older. Joel 2:28 states: "Your old men will dream dreams." One man wrote: "I get up each morning, dust off my wits, pick up the paper, and read the obits. If my name is missing, I know I'm not dead, so I eat a good breakfast and go back to bed."

D. You're younger than you think:

1. Moses was 80 when God called him to deliver Israel.

2. Michelangelo was writing poetry and designing buildings up to the time of his death at 90. He painted the ceiling of the Sistine Chapel on his back on a scaffold at nearly 90.

3. Von Goethe wrote a part of *Faust* at 60 and finished it at 82.

4. Webster wrote his monumental dictionary at 70.

5. Ogilvie, the translator of Homer and Virgil, was unacquainted with Latin and Greek until he was past 50.

6. Tennyson published "Crossing the Bar" at 83.

7. Verdi produced the famous piece "Ave Maria" at 85.

8. John Wesley preached for 40 years; produced 400 books; knew 10 languages; at 86 he complained that he was unable to preach more than twice a day.

9. I have a friend whose father is a minister. Last year he earned his doctorate—he was 76.

II. Joseph Had a God-Given Dream (37:5, 9).

    A. The two dreams confirmed that the dreams came from God and were guaranteed by God's promise (see also 41:32 for the significance of two dreams).

    B. The problem of self-contrived dreams: Ecclesiastes 5:7 says, "Much dreaming and many words are meaningless. Therefore stand in awe of God." Self-contrived dreams are self-serving. Joseph did not make up his dream. Such action would have demonstrated the height of arrogance. God does not promise to bless our dreams. He promises to bless the dreams He imparts to us as we learn to walk in those dreams.

    C. How to have a God-dream for your life: Look at your talents and gifts and form a dream for your life based on what God has given you. Also be open to God leading you into an area of ministry and service. God has both "gifts and callings" (Romans 11:29).

III. Joseph Knew How to Make His Dreams Become Reality.

It takes faith and patience to turn dreams into reality (Hebrews 6:12).

    A. *Faith.* It took tremendous faith for him to share his dream with his family. He was only 17. He knew the possibility of being misunderstood, but he believed deeply in what God had shown him. You have to keep faith in the face of misunderstanding. Believe in your dream when no one else understands or supports you. Even Jesus' own family thought He had lost His mind. Not until after His resurrection did His own family follow Him.

Illustration

Lao-Tse was a crippled Chinese woman who opened a home for cripples in China on the site of a pond where crippled children were once thrown to their deaths. In that small room, her faith worked through her love to save children. She inspired others and, as a result, received finances by which she was able to help those in desperate need. Think of it—a cripple setting up a home for cripples.

She said, "My religion is to think the unthinkable thought, to speak the ineffable word, to do the impossible deed and to walk the impossible way." At her funeral, she was described as one who possessed "the miracle of a healthy mind" and an "illumined face." She had a dream from God, and it became a reality because of the promise of God.

B. *Patience.* This means to be long-suffering and to be undismayed by difficulties. Patience is faith in the fact of difficulties. Joseph saw God at work even in the most adverse circumstances (Genesis 50:20). "Through many dangers, toils and snares," Joseph's dream would be fulfilled. Perseverance is required because all dreamers must be tested. He spent 13 years in prison before his dream reached fulfillment.

God's purpose in patience is to bring us into greater conformity to the image of Christ. "Perseverance must finish its work so that you may be mature and complete, not lacking anything" (James 1:4).

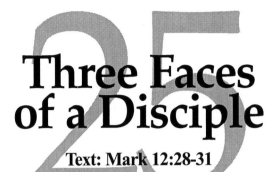

Three Faces
of a Disciple
Text: Mark 12:28-31

Years ago when you identified yourself as a Christian, people had a basic sense of what you meant. Although in a survey of 13,000 a large percentage of Americans identified themselves as Christian, the word *Christian* is used in a variety of ways. Sometimes we feel like asking, "Will the real Christians please stand up?"

In the '70s we started clarifying the term by adding the qualifier, *born-again*. When presidential hopeful Jimmy Carter said he was a born-again Christian, very few people knew what he meant except for one reporter, Wesley Pippert, who attended seminary along the way. Soon everyone on radio and TV talked about being born-again. In search for greater clarity, we began describing ourselves as Spirit-filled Christians. But soon, even that became controversial. Did we mean "Spirit-filled reformed" or "Spirit-filled charismatic"? Then, we added our eschatological perspectives on the return of Christ in relation to the Great Tribulation and found ourselves majoring on minors and drowning in theological lingo. Today, the term *Evangelical Christian* is widely used, but new studies show it is getting less popular among Americans because it is associated with certain political persuasions.

Long before we used all these labels, laden with adjectives, we were simply known as disciples of Jesus Christ (Acts 11:26). The question before us is simply, Are we disciples of Jesus Christ? What is a disciple? The word *disciple* simply means a "student." More specifically, a disciple is a follower (Matthew 4:19), learner (11:29), and an imitator of Christ (Luke 6:40).

Everywhere Jesus went, He called disciples. The word appears nearly 300 times in the New Testament. He described disciples as people experiencing a radical change in their personalities, priorities and passions as a direct result of His lordship in their lives. Here are some major qualities of disciples:

- Self-denial (Luke 9:23)
- Supreme love for Christ (14:26)
- Kingdom responsibility (v. 27)
- Kingdom values (v. 33)
- Submit to Scripture (John 8:31, 32)
- Love for others (13:34, 35)
- Produce spiritual fruit (15:8)

The great commandments give us three aspects of discipleship so that we can truly change our world for Christ:

I.   Love God.

The *Shema* (which means "hear" in Hebrew) of Judaism, the Great Commandment, was written on a small scroll and was kept in phylacteries on the hands or foreheads (Deuteronomy 6:4-9). It was, and is, also placed in the *mezuzah*, a small box placed on the door of every Jewish home. In Jesus' time, the rabbis had expanded the Law into thousands of laws for the people to accurately interpret the law of Moses. Jesus, on the other hand, reduced the Law down to its most basic meaning— love the Lord your God. Here is a love that is all-encompassing, involving the total person. Notice that we are to love God with all our . . .

A. Spirit: our God-consciousness
B. Mind: our intellect, will and emotion
C. Body: our strength and the faculty of our five senses.

II. Love Your Neighbor.

Jesus always points to the horizontal dimension of religion when He speaks of the vertical dimension. Our relationship with God is reflected in our interpersonal relationships. James confronts our hypocrisy by saying that we bless God yet curse man, who is made in God's image (James 3:9). Here are three practical steps to loving your neighbor:

A. Go to people when they are in need, as the Good Samaritan went to where the injured man was and helped him (Luke 10:25-37).

B. Accept people as they are without passing judgment on them, just as God has accepted us with unconditional love (Romans 15:7).

C. Get out of your comfort zone and meet people who are different from you so that you can learn to appreciate the diversity of God's creation in us. And get out of the church and into the world and become a friend of sinners as Jesus was. We can't win people to Christ unless we build relationships with those who are lost so that we can minister to them. Jesus went to the home of Zacchaeus for lunch first, then He ministered salvation to him (Luke 19:1-10).

III. Love Yourself.

A. Some argue as to whether or not this is part of the commandment. What does it mean? Certainly Christ is not calling for narcissism, self-centeredness or self-preoccupation. Nor is He advocating the modern-day gospel of self-esteem, which asserts that the answer to all human suffering consists of a good dose of self-esteem.

B. Perhaps what Jesus calls for is an accurate sense of self-awareness. And, after all, what are we to do with ourselves?

1. Deny yourself (Luke 9:23).
2. Dedicate yourself (Romans 12:1, 2).
3. Discipline yourself (1 Corinthians 9:24-27).
4. Develop yourself (2 Timothy 2:15).
5. Die to yourself (Galatians 2:20).

Closing: Keep your faith in Christ simple. His yoke is easy and His burden is light (Matthew 11:30). He gives us three powerful principles to be world-changers: Love the Lord your God, love your neighbor, and love yourself.

The Spirit Is Willing, the Flesh Is Weak

Text: Matthew 26:36-41

Sir Edwin Arnold, author of *The Light of Asia,* when speaking to the students at Harvard College, said, "In 1776 you conquered your fathers. In 1861 you conquered your brothers. Now the next great victory is to conquer yourselves."

His words provide a more important challenge to us as believers. The greatest war we face is a battle within ourselves. We all identify with the statement, "I've had more trouble with myself than any other man I've ever met."

Now to be sure, we confront outward forces: Satan (Ephesians 6:12) and the world system (1 John 2:15-17), but the greatest struggle lies within. Paul identifies it clearly in Romans 7:15-25.

The inward battle involves a battle with the flesh. What is the flesh, anyway? The Greek word Paul uses is *sarx*—the sin nature; the nature of man devoid of the Spirit of God. In Freudian terms, it is the *id* that seeks to avoid pain, relieve tension, and obtain pleasure—biological, instinctual urges that seek expression regardless of social or divine boundaries.

- Inherited from Adam (Romans 5:12)
- Oriented toward self-fulfillment (1 John 2:16)
- Rebellious toward God and His law (Romans 8:6-8)
- Results in carnal living (Galatians 5:19-21)

Illustration

The flesh always wants to be first. Occasionally we are like terrible-tempered Lucy in the *Peanuts* comic strip. Lucy comes into the room where her little brother, Linus, is watching TV. He says to her, "I was here first, so I get to watch what I want to watch." Without a word, Lucy marches to the TV and flips the channel to her program. Linus protests, "Hey! You can't do that." Assuming her know-it-all stance, Lucy says, "In the 19th chapter of the Book of Matthew it says, 'The first will be last, and the last will be first.'" Linus mutters to himself, "I'll bet Matthew didn't have an older sister!"

Is there a way out? Victory over the flesh comes through the power of the Holy Spirit (Galatians 5:16, 17). The fact of the matter is, we do not always conquer the flesh; it conquers us. We've all been there, haven't we? We said yes when we vowed to say no; we yielded when we resolved to stand our ground; we surrendered when we were determined to fight.

The disciples of Jesus struggled with the flesh in Gethsemane. Christ knew the force of the inward battle between the flesh and spirit and admonished them to victory that night. What can we learn from their experience?

I.   Know Your Vulnerability.

A.   The spirit is willing, the flesh is weak (Matthew 26:41). Remember: "Pride goes before destruction" (Proverbs 16:18). Paul said, "If you think you are standing firm, be careful that you don't fall" (1 Corinthians 10:12).

B.   We all possess an Achilles' heel. In Greek mythology, Achilles' mother held him by the heel and dipped him in the river Styx to make him invincible in battle. However, the place where she held him by the heel remained untouched by the water of the Styx, leaving a vulnerable, unprotected area. In a battle, a warrior struck him in his heel with an arrow, and he bled to death.

As Mike Wallace of *60 Minutes* introduced a story about Nazi Adolf Eichmann, a principal architect of the Holocaust, he posed a central question at the program's outset: "How is it possible . . . for a man to act as Eichmann acted?" Was he a monster? A madman? Or was he perhaps something even more terrifying: was he normal?" The startling answer to Wallace's shocking question came in an interview with Yehiel Dinur, a concentration camp survivor who testified against Eichmann at the Nuremberg trials. A film clip from Eichmann's 1961 trial showed Dinur walking in to the courtroom, stopping short and seeing Eichmann for the first time since the Nazi had sent him to Auschwitz 18 years earlier. Dinur began to sob uncontrollably, then fainted, collapsing in a heap on the floor. Was Dinur overcome by hatred? Fear? Horrid memories? No, it was none of these. Rather, as Dinur explained to Wallace, all at once he realized Eichmann was not the godlike army officer who had sent so many to their deaths. This Eichmann was an ordinary man. "I was afraid about myself," said Dinur. "I saw that I am capable to do this. I am . . . exactly like him." Wallace's summation of Dinur's terrible discovery—"Eichmann is in all of us"—is a terrifying statement, but it indeed captures man's sin nature (From Chuck Colson, *The Danger of Being Normal*).

Illustration

II. Pay Attention.

    A.   *Watch* is a military word invoking images of watchmen guarding a city from its walls. In the Old Testament, prophets were called *watchmen* (spiritual watchmen). Thomas Carlyle said: "For every person who can handle prosperity, there are a hundred who can handle adversity."

    B.   The invasion of Pearl Harbor on December 7, 1941, was a day Roosevelt called "a date which will forever live in infamy." We were simply caught off guard, and the results were devastating.

C. Satan is unrelenting. Luke 4:13 records, "When the devil had finished all this tempting, he left him until an opportune time." The devil always comes back. Just because we win a spiritual battle, it doesn't mean we won't face the same battle later. Victory is not a single event but a process. So we need to be on our guard when the Enemy returns with another battle.

III. Keep in Touch.

A. Keep in touch with your source of strength. "Pray so that you will not fall into temptation" (Matthew 26:41). He does not say prayer will keep us from temptation but, rather, enable us to overcome temptation by giving us a discerning spirit and by giving us strength.

B. The only ministry request Christ's disciples ever made that we know of was, "Lord, teach us to pray" (Luke 11:1). Jesus had a habit of disappearing, of slipping away privately to pray, and then emerging with tremendous power. They wanted to know the secret of prayer.

Illustration

Billy Graham was once asked what constituted the success of his meetings. He said, "Three things. One, prayer. Two, prayer. Three, prayer."

IV. Get Up When You Fall (Luke 22:31-34).

Peter learned how to get back up after his denial of Christ (see John 21). Jesus asked him, "Do you love me?" Then He told Peter, "Feed my sheep" (see vv. 15-17). You see, God is the God of new beginnings. He gives a new song (Psalm 40:3), a new heart (Ezekiel 36:26) and a new creation (2 Corinthians 5:17). He is the God who makes "all things new" (Revelation 21:5, *NKJV*). Truly, His mercies are new every morning (Lamentations 3:22, 23). Make this declaration to the Enemy of your soul if you have fallen: "Do not gloat over me, my enemy! Though I have fallen, I will rise" (Micah 7:8).

As Thomas Edison's plant caught fire and burned to the ground, he stood along with his wife and watched as so many costly experiments perished in the flames. As the flames lit up the night sky, Edison turned to his wife and his son Charles and said, "Isn't it wonderful?" "Isn't what wonderful?" they responded. "Isn't it wonderful? All our mistakes are being burned up in the fire. Tomorrow morning we can start over brand new!" Within two weeks, a new plant was under construction, and it wasn't long until he invented the phonograph.

Illustration

Perhaps there are some things you would like to put in the fire of the Holy Spirit and start over brand new.

Repent and Live!

Text: Ezekiel 8:30-32

E very field of study—mathematics, science, psychology, sociology, theology—is characterized by a unique language. The mastery of any field of study requires, first of all, the student to learn the language of that particular field of study.

When we read the Bible we encounter the language of faith. Powerful, life-changing words appear throughout its pages. One of the most important words in the Bible, which desperately needs rediscovering in our times, is the word *repentance.* From Genesis to Revelation, through the mouths of prophets, priests and poets, God calls us to repentance.

J. Edwin Orr notes that *repentance* is the first word of the gospel (Matthew 4:17). The first of the 95 theses Martin Luther nailed to the Wittenberg church door read, "When our Lord and Master Jesus Christ said 'repent,' He willed that the entire life of believers be one of repentance."

When you hear the word *repentance,* or the imperative *repent,* what comes to your mind? Do you picture Jonah, fresh out of the belly of a whale, walking into Nineveh covered with seaweed, bearing the odor of a fish, declaring, "Repent!"? Or maybe you picture

John the Baptist, in the Judean wilderness, dressed in camel's hair, with eyes of fire, confronting everyone from religious aristocrats to the common man with the challenge, "Repent!" Or maybe you see a man in a downtown park carrying a sign over his shoulder bearing the inscription, "Repent!"

We ask ourselves, "What does repentance mean?" *To repent* (*metanoeo*) literally means "to perceive afterward" (*meta*, "after," implying change; *noeo*, "to perceive," from *nous*, the mind or seat of moral reflection). *Repentance*, then, means to change your mind or your purpose. In the Bible, repentance is always used to mean changing one's mind for the better. More specifically, we turn away from sin and turn toward God. Thus, repentance means a change of mind, a change of direction and a change of behavior. W.E. Vines defines *repentance* as "the adjustment of the moral and spiritual vision and thinking to (that of) the mind of God, which is designed to have a transforming effect upon the life."

Jesus' parable of the Prodigal Son (Luke 15:11-31) provides us the clearest picture of repentance. He leaves his father and, by doing so, turns his back to his father. In the distant country, he finds himself bankrupt from sinful living, tending pigs and eating the corn husks given to the pigs. There "he came to his senses" (a change of mind) and says, "I will go to my father" (a change of purpose) and then turns around and travels home (a change of direction) and, ultimately, there is a change of destination, for he arrives home. Any person who repents of sin and changes direction ultimately changes his or her destination.

Repentance concerns every person. God calls both the sinner and saint, the unbeliever and the believer in Christ, to repentance. Not only is repentance fundamental in salvation, it is also fundamental to spiritual maturity and abundant joy (Isaiah 30:15; Luke 13:3; Acts 2:38; 2 Corinthians 7:10; 2 Peter 3:9).

God's grace enables us to repent. It is no accident that we feel convicted of our sins, constrained to turn around, and challenged to turn back to God. We, however, must choose to respond to His

grace and repent. There are those who express partial repentance—
Like *Pharaoh*, who hardened his heart at the command of God; or
King Saul, who publicly admitted his sin but privately still sought
David's death; or *Judas*, who was grieved that he betrayed Christ
but failed to turn back to God.

When we repent, God blesses: "If my people, who are called by
name, will humble themselves and pray and seek my face and turn
from their wicked ways, then will I hear from heaven and will forgive their sin and will heal their land" (2 Chronicles 7:14).

EZEKIEL'S CHALLENGE

The historical background of Ezekiel was the Babylonian Exile,
which lasted 70 years. There were three deportations of Jews to
Babylon (modern Iraq): (1) 605 B.C.—Daniel and others; (2) 597
B.C.—Ezekiel and 10,000 Jews; (3) 586 B.C.—destruction of
Jerusalem and the Temple, final deportation. Ezekiel ministered to
the Jews during their exile in Babylon. His name means "God
strengthens." His father was a priest and he was influenced greatly
by Jeremiah. Exiled at age 25, he began his ministry around age 30.
Not only was he educated in the customs of his own people, but his
writings also reflect a tremendous knowledge of international historical affairs as well as others customs, trades and literature. He
often used illustrative sermons to powerfully convey his message.
His message was straightforward: Repent and live! (18:32).

I. Repentance Is Both Corporate and Personal (v. 30).

   A. *National.* "O house of Israel . . ." The United States finds
       itself in need of repentance of racism and social injustice.
       Also, it needs to repent of its immorality, corruption of our
       young, and 1.6 million abortions per year.

   B. *Personal.* "I will judge . . . each one according to his ways"
       (v. 30). Note verse 4: "The soul who sins is the one who
       will die" (see also vv. 19, 20). Ezekiel has been called the
       prophet of personal responsibility. Human behavior is . . .

       1. Free

       2. Responsible

       3. Accountable.

    C. *The blame game.* We can make the mistake of blaming the government, our past, parents, peers, environmental conditions. We need to practice self-examination and take personal responsibility.

Illustration

Toward the end of the 19th century, Swedish chemist Alfred Nobel awoke one morning to read his own obituary in the local newspaper: "Alfred Nobel, the inventor of dynamite, who died yesterday, devised a way for more people to be killed in a war than ever before, and he died a very rich man." Actually, it was Alfred's brother who had died; a reporter botched the epitaph. The account had a profound effect on Alfred Nobel. He decided that he wanted to be known for something other than inventing the means for killing people in war and for amassing great wealth in the process. So he initiated the Nobel Prize, the award for scientists and writers who foster peace. He said, "Every man ought to have the chance to correct his epitaph in midstream and write a new one" (*Is It Real When It Doesn't Work?* Doug Murren and Barb Shurin, cited in Larson, *Illustrations for Preaching & Teaching*).

II. Repentance Involves Both a Turning Away and a Turning Toward God (v. 30b).

    A. We often leave out the second dimension. As a result, repentance takes on a negative definition—getting rid of something, putting off, crucifying the flesh, giving up. There are Christians who live a negative life based on such a notion of repentance. But God never takes anything out of our lives that He does not replace with something far greater. The Prodigal Son was no better off for deciding he no longer wanted to be working on a pig farm. His life improved only when he took positive action and went home where he found complete restoration of his dignity.

B. We have to put off the old before we can put on the new blessings God has for us (Ephesians 4:22-24).

C. God desires to fill us, not to empty us. We empty ourselves through repentance so that we can be filled with all the fullness of God (3:19). The Christian life is . . .

   1. A plus, rather than a minus
   2. An addition, rather than a subtraction
   3. A positive, rather than a negative
   4. A multiplication, rather than a division
   5. An enlargement rather than a reduction!

III. Repentance Is Both Internal and External (v. 31).

"Rid yourselves of all the offenses you have committed, and get a new heart and a new spirit." He uses new-covenant language in 36:26, 27. Notice God says "I will." Only God can give us a new heart. When we repent, we submit ourselves to the transforming work of the Spirit, who removes the heart of stone (resistant, rebellious, stubborn) and gives us a heart of flesh (soft, pliable, yielded). Look at the facets of repentance that involve the total person:

A. *Emotionally*, we feel convicted of our sins—remorseful that we violated the law of God and grieved His heart.

B. *Intellectually*, we submit our minds to the law of God and agree with God's Word that sin is sin.

C. *Volitionally*, we chose to return to God and turn away from our sins.

D. *Behaviorally*, we live out our repentance by a new lifestyle.

When Jim Vaus, the underworld figure, came to Christ in 1949, he spent many weeks looking up people he had offended, injured, and stolen from. He returned everything he could and apologized to all he had offended.

Illustration

The prophetic words of God are replete with promise—Repent and live! God says, "I take no pleasure in the death of anyone" (18:32). He promises life—abundant and eternal. In Eden, God says, "If you eat of the tree you will die" (see Genesis 2:17). At Calvary, God says, "If you partake of this tree, the cross of Christ, you will live." We partake of Christ when we repent and believe.

To an
Unknown God

Text: Acts 17:16-34

G od is alive and well in America. Conclusive research shows that 90 percent of adults questioned said they believe in God. When asked if they believed that "there is only one true God, who is holy and perfect and who created the world and rules it today," 74 percent said yes.

Unfortunately, for some, God doesn't make much difference in their lives. For example, when making decisions, especially about moral issues, very few people turn to God for guidance. Instead, we look to ourselves for such guidance. Americans usually choose which commandments to believe and tend to think of God as "a general principle of life" or as a "distant and pale reflection of the God of our forefathers" (Collins, *Christian Counseling for People Helpers*).

A parallel exists between our times and the times of Athens when Paul visited the city during his second missionary journey. By the first century, Athens' political and economic power had vanished. It remained, however, a center for learning and art, featuring a great university that continued drawing men seeking knowledge.

Furthermore, Athens was filled with idols to the Greek gods. Some said in Athens it was easier to meet a god than a man. The religion of Greece consisted of a glorification of human attributes and the powers of nature. It lacked any moral power to shape human character, relationships and society. It reflects the humanism and New Ageism of our day.

Athens also existed as the noted center of philosophy, featuring great thinkers like Socrates and Aristotle. Aristotle defined *philosophy* as "the science which considers truth." The Athenians lost their work ethic, preferring rather to discuss new ideas, relish in past glory, and enjoy latest novelties.

Paul was alone in Athens for a short time. While there, he began to preach and dialogue with Jews and God-fearing Greeks about Jesus Christ. He also spoke daily in the marketplace, called the *agora*, to anyone who would listen. The *agora* featured a round podium in the center of the shops, affording anyone the opportunity to deliver a public discourse.

The two groups of philosophers called Stoics and Epicureans disputed with Paul, calling him a "babbler" (v. 18). The word *babbler* literally means "seed-picker," which originally referred to birds gathering seeds and scraps, then referred to someone who collects ideas here and there as a plagiarist whose learning is secondhand and undigested. They accused him of advocating false gods because he spoke of Jesus and the Resurrection.

He was then invited to a meeting of the Areopagus, where they asked him to explain his new teaching. The Areopagus (hill of Ares, the Greek god of thunder and war, later called Mars by the Romans) originally housed the Court or Council of Athens, which governed a Greek city-state but, in Paul's time, related only to matters of religion, philosophy and morality. They regarded themselves as custodians of philosophical tradition and teaching.

Paul delivered a masterful message, "To an Unknown God," taken from the inscription he noticed on one of their many altars. Other Greek writers in extra-Biblical literature confirm such inscriptions on altars in Athens. The Greeks were fearful of offending any deity by failing to give him due honor, so they erected altars to unknown gods.

What did Paul do that day that teaches us how to speak to people about God?

I.   He Affirmed Their Religious Pursuits.

"Men of Athens! I see that in every way you are very religious [superstitious]" (v. 22). Paul puts his finger on a universal need and intuition—the need to know God and to enjoy His fellowship.

II.   He Acknowledged Their Spiritual Confusion.

"What you worship as something unknown I am going to proclaim to you" (v. 23).

A.   Their vision of God was out of focus as He is today with so many. Who is God? What is He like? Paul preached to bring God into focus so that He would no longer be unknown to the Athenians.

B.   Jesus made a similar statement to the woman at the well, "You Samaritans worship what you do not know." Yet, He said, "The time is coming and has now come when the true worshipers will worship the Father in spirit and truth, for they are the kind of worshipers the Father seeks. God is spirit, and his worshipers must worship in spirit and in truth" (John 4:22-24). In other words, worship must be based on the knowledge of who God is, not on our own inventions of God.

C.   What happens to us when God is unknown?

1.   *We lose our sense of identity.* We become cosmic orphans in the universe, unable to answer the larger questions of purpose, meaning and destiny.

2.   *We fall into idolatry.* We fashion God in our own image.

3.   *We are estranged from God and experience cultural degeneracy.* We lose the absolute and practice moral relativity.

4.   *We feel spiritually estranged from God.*

III. He Announced the True and Living God (17:24-31).

A. *God is Creator* (v. 24). God made the world and everything in it. He is Lord of heaven and earth. He does not live in temples made by hands. Since God made all things, He cannot be worshiped by what our hands make—such as idols. Man seems bent on worshiping what his hands make.

B. *God is Sustainer* (v. 25).

1. *God is not served by human hands.* In reality, God serves us. He provides for our every need. He sends rain on the just and the unjust, which is common grace (Matthew 5:45). Christ said, "The Son of Man did not come to be served, but to serve, and to give his life as a ransom for many" (Mark 10:45).

2. *God is self-existent* ("as if he needed anything").

3. *God gives life and breath to all men.* He sustains the universe (Hebrews 1:3). Consider the delicate balance of our atmosphere of oxygen, nitrogen, carbon dioxide. If the oxygen content were raised from 20 percent to 32 percent, all the combustible substances on earth would burst into flames.

C. *God is Sovereign* (vv. 26-28).

1. *God created all men from one man (blood).* This affirms the brotherhood of man.

2. *God ordained the nations and historical movements.* This does not mean that God orchestrated all historical developments such as the Holocaust, slavery, Iraq's brutal invasion of Kuwait, or China's abusive violation of human rights. It does mean, however, that ultimately God is in control of human history, and He will bring history to a rendezvous with Himself at a place called *Armageddon.* All history will culminate with an act of divine judgment and redemption by which all things shall be restored (Acts 3:21) and all things gathered "together under one head, even Christ" (Ephesians 1:10).

3. *God's purpose in all things is that we might seek Him*

and find Him. He is near (imminent). Paul quotes the
Cretan poet Epimenides (c. 600 B.C.): "In him we live
and move and have our being." He adds the words of
the Cilician poet Aratus (c. 315-240 B.C.), "We are his
offspring."

D. *God is Redeemer* (vv. 29-31).

    1. God commands us to repent of our ignorance and idol-
atry. To repent is to change our minds and, consequently, our behavior.

    2. God will judge the world through Jesus Christ. "The
man" (v. 31) is actually "the Son of Man" according to
the Old Testament prophet Daniel in 7:13, 14: "In my
vision at night I looked, and there before me was one
like a son of man, coming with the clouds of heaven. He
approached the Ancient of Days and was led into his
presence. He was given authority, glory and sovereign
power; all peoples, nations and men of every language
worshiped him. His dominion is an everlasting dominion that will not pass away, and his kingdom is one that
will never be destroyed." Jesus described His second
coming in the same way (Matthew 24:27-31).

    3. The risen Christ is the only hope for the world. Christ
was judged in our place (2 Corinthians 5:21). He is the
risen Lord.

Billy Graham, in addressing the Christian Workers Conference,
said: "I was in Russia preaching before the communists fell. We had
gone to a number of cities in Russia and I had preached the gospel,
and a clergyman was sitting beside me in the car. We were on the
way to the airport, and I said, 'You've heard me preach in these various cities. Do you have any suggestions?' He said, 'I have one.
Preach the Resurrection more. Without the Resurrection, the Cross
does not have meaning.'"

Illustration

IV. **The People's Response (vv. 32-34).**

    Their responses varied as with all preaching:

A. *Those who ridiculed*—laughed off the whole issue

B. *Those who wanted to hear more*

C. *Those who believed*—Dionysius of the Areopagus and a woman named Damaris, as well as a number of others

Closing: Paul's sermon has been described by some as a colossal failure. They suggest that Paul learned the hard way that preaching to the intellect avails nothing. They note that Jesus is never mentioned by name in the sermon nor is the cross of Christ. His ministry produced neither a riot nor a revival. We possess no record of a great church being established in Athens at that time, although tradition later speaks of Dionysius as the church's pastor. However, Luke only recorded highlights of the sermon. I believe Paul preached the only gospel he ever preached: "Jesus Christ and him crucified" (1 Corinthians 2:2). Paul was wise enough to communicate the gospel in the language of the people of his day, and we need to follow his example to reach our generation for Christ.

On Eagles' Wings

Text: Exodus 19:3-6

Throughout Scripture, God reveals Himself to us through the use of metaphors. In Exodus, God says to Israel, "I carried you on eagles' wings and brought you to myself" (v. 4).

In what ways does God carry us like an eagle carries her young? The female golden eagle best fits this description. Eagles live in most of the Northern Hemisphere. They are a symbol of power and courage because of their large size, aerial skills, and inaccessibility of nests in wild, mountainous country. Their nests are usually built on cliff ledges, although some build in trees. They keep the same nest, adding new sticks every year until nests become as large as 6 feet in diameter and 5 feet high. They produce few eggs and usually hatch and rear only two nestlings. The male hunts food and brings it to the nest, and the female feeds. As nestlings mature, the female hunts as well. The female grows up to 3 feet in length with a 7-foot wingspan. Males are smaller, as with most birds of prey, and fly upward up to 85 mph and downward up to 140 mph. The eagle is a symbol used for certain Roman legions; France used it under

Napoleon, and it is the great seal of the U.S.. Eagles exhibit grandeur in flight, rise above the clouds, transcend dangers below, build nests on high, mate for life, travel independently (not in flocks), and provide for and protect family.

Occasionally, in Scripture, God and His people are compared to eagles. Not only does God tell Israel, "I carried you out of Egypt on eagles' wings," but He "shielded him [Israel] and cared for him; he guarded him as the apple of his eye, like an eagle that stirs up its nest and hovers over its young, that spreads its wings to catch them and carries them on its pinions" (Deuteronomy 32:10, 11).

Stirring the nest is an interesting process. The eagle constructs the nest from thorns, jagged stones and pointed sticks, then covers the interior with feathers, wool and fur from animals she has killed. Thus, the nest is soft and comfortable for the nestlings. However, the time will come when she will stir up the nest. She removes the wool, feathers and fur, picking it out piece by piece and throwing it to the wind. The now-developing eagles find themselves pricked by the sharp edges of the sticks and thorns. She no longer brings food and places it in their mouths. It doesn't take long for them to venture out of the comfort of the nest, to spread their wings and soar to become what they were destined to become (Isaiah 40:31).

When God says, "I carried you on eagles' wings," He is reminding us that He cares about us as an eagle cares for her young. Somehow we need to get in touch again with the care of God. This is the essence of faith according to Hebrews 11:6: "Believe that he exists and that he rewards those who earnestly seek him." God exists and He cares. In Isaiah 25:4 we read: "[God has] been a refuge for the poor, a refuge for the needy in his distress, a shelter from the storm and a shade from the heat." Peter tells us, "He cares for you" (1 Peter 5:7).

The God of creation, revealed in the Bible, who appeared in Jesus Christ, is not a God who lives far removed from us, somewhere in this vast universe. Some time ago, a popular song was released by Bette Midler that said, "God is watching us, from a distance." Nothing could be further from the truth. To the contrary, I say with the psalmist, "The Lord is at my right hand, I shall not be moved" (16:8, KJV).

God numbers the hairs on our heads. He knows when a sparrow falls to the ground. He knows the way each of us takes, and He cares. He says, "Fear not. . . . When you pass through the waters, I will be with you; and when you pass through the rivers, they will not sweep over you. When you walk through the fire, you will not be burned; the flames will not set you ablaze. For I am the Lord, your God, the Holy One of Israel, your Savior" (Isaiah 43:1-3).

I.   On Eagles' Wings, God Carried Them out of Egypt.
     A. Egypt represented an impossible situation. Without the intervention of God, Israel would be hopelessly bound in slavery in Egypt. God asks Abraham (Genesis 18:14), and Jeremiah answers (32:17). Jesus reminds us, "With men this is impossible, but with God all things are possible" (Matthew 19:26). We need to put three words in our vocabulary: *God is able!* (Ephesians 3:20).
     B. Egypt also represents captivity to sin (Romans 3:23). Like Israel, we are redeemed by the blood of the Lamb and the power of God.

I visited a man in the hospital suffering with cancer. Two feet of his intestines had been removed, and he was scheduled to go out of state to see a specialist. After I prayed for him he said, "All my life I've been a sinner." I said, "This is true of us all." Then he said, "I guess if we weren't all sinners, there would have been no reason for Him to come."

Illustration

II. On Eagles' Wings, God Carried Them Through the Wilderness
     A. I wish I could tell you that the wilderness is not a part of life, but that would not be the truth. But God carries His people through the wilderness—the wilderness of sickness, discouragement, death of a loved one, financial stress, marital pressure, family problems, and ministry challenges. God

does not always immediately take us *out of* our wilderness experience, but He always brings us *through*.

B.   Israel faced two wilderness experiences—the wilderness of faith en route to the Promised Land and, later, the wilderness of disobedience for 40 years.

C.   The wilderness is a part of life (John 16:33). God used the wilderness experiences . . .

1.   *To display His power.* He alone would bring them through.

2.   *To defeat their enemies.* Psalm 136:16-20 declares, "To Him who led his people through the desert . . . who struck down great kings . . . and killed mighty kings . . . Sihon king of the Amorites . . . and Og king of Bashan."

3.   *To speak His word in undisturbed solitude.* In the wilderness, Elijah heard God's "still small voice" (1 Kings 19:12, *NKJV*).

4.   *To test them.* The wilderness prepared Israel for conquest. God also tested them to teach them to trust Him (see Deuteronomy 8:2, 3).

D.   The God of the wilderness still provides . . .

1.   Manna from heaven

2.   Water from the rock

3.   The pillar of fire at night to protect

4.   The cloud by day to guide

5.   Shekinah glory to fill our hearts as He filled the Tabernacle to remind us that God is in the midst of His people, and He will bring them through.

III. On Eagles' Wings, God Carried Them Into the Promised Land.

A.   God always directs us toward His promise for our lives— "a land flowing with milk and honey" (Exodus 3:8; see also John 10:10). The Promised Land isn't perfect. There were enemies to face, battles to fight, temptations to conquer, cities to build, vineyards to plant.

B. God brings us out of sin for the sole purpose of bringing us into a life of promise. The promise represents life lived in the fullness of His presence and blessing. The promise is connected with God's purpose for our lives. The blessing abides where His will is obeyed and His purpose fulfilled.

Closing: Perhaps you need to be carried by God. You are not alone in your situation. God knows where you are, and He cares. He has a promise for you: "I will carry you on eagles' wings out of impossible situations, through the wilderness, and into the fullness of My purpose for your life."

Going Home

Text: Joshua 1:1-9

Most children think of running away from home sometime during their childhood; some even try it. They dream of being independent; having no rules; imagining life as one big party.

As a boy of about 6, I decided to run away from home one day. So I boldly announced my plan to my parents. To my surprise, they walked me to the front door and bade me farewell. As soon as I hit the street, I began to feel the loneliness of having left the safety and security of home. I only went a short distance down the street, barely out of their sight, when I decided I made a big mistake and started back. Coincidentally, I also began to have a stomachache. When I got back home, I told my parents my stomach hurt. Of course, they thought I was only looking for attention. A few hours later, I was doubled over in pain. They rushed me to the hospital. Within an hour, I was in emergency surgery due to a twisted intestine on the verge of rupturing. Needless to say, since that time I've never been too keen on running away from home.

The basic problem with humanity today—the root cause of our social, economic, political, racial and spiritual problems—is the fact that we, like rebellious children, have run away from home. Our first parents, Adam and Eve, did. They decided that they would try life out from under God's rules, and they ran away from God. We've been running ever since, living life in a foreign land, exiled from our homeland.

We can identify with ancient Judah when they were exiled from their homeland. The prophets forewarned them that Babylon would invade them if they persisted in their sin. And their prophecies came to pass. In 588 B.C., Nebuchadnezzar's army laid siege to Jerusalem. Two years later, the city fell, and the people of Judah were deported to Babylon. The city was burned to the ground. The Temple of Solomon was destroyed, the holy articles confiscated. For 70 years they were in Babylon, longing to go home. The psalmist expressed their pain in 137:1-4: "By the rivers of Babylon we sat and wept when we remembered Zion. There on the poplars we hung our harps, for there our captors asked us for songs, our tormentors demanded songs of joy; they said, 'Sing us one of the songs of Zion!' How can we sing the songs of the Lord while in a foreign land?"

Ezekiel (whose name means "God is strong") was a priest who grew up as a young man in Babylon along with his exiled people. He announced their homecoming. God would go to any extreme to get His people back (36:24-27). This message contains vital truths about God's commitment to us:

I.   Promise: "I Will Gather You."

A. *The God of ingathering.* There is a harvest today in the world: John 4:35 says, "Do you not say, 'Four months more and then the harvest'? I tell you, open your eyes and look at the fields! They are ripe for harvest."

B. *The ultimate gathering will come in heaven.* Matthew 24:31 says, "And he will send his angels with a loud trumpet call, and they will gather his elect from the four winds, from one end of the heavens to the other."

C. *The God who searches for us.* The Christian testimony is not, "I found the Lord," but rather, "The Lord found me."

God is not interested in casting us away, but He is gathering us in, as seen in the parables of Luke 15: the lost sheep, lost coin, and lost son.

Jewish Legend of Creation. God prepares to create man. Before creating Adam, He took into His counsel the four great angels who encircle His throne. After revealing His plan to create man in His own image with the full powers of intellect, will and emotion, the Angel of Justice objected, "Do not create him, for he will commit all acts of injustice and cruelty against his fellowman." The Angel of Truth objected, "Do not create him, for he will be dishonest and deceitful in his relations with others." The Angel of Holiness objected, "Do not create him, for he will indulge his carnal nature and violate Your laws." Finally, the Angel of Mercy spoke: "Create him, for in the day that he sins and departs from the way of justice, truth and holiness, I shall go to him, take him by the hand and bring him back to You."

Illustration

II. Cleansing: "I Will Sprinkle Clean Water on You."

A. What a magnificent promise: cleansing. This is our most desperate need today. Sin leaves us unclean, guilt-ridden, carrying a sense of shame.

B. Karl Menninger asked, "Whatever became of sin?" Sin went to the psychiatrist and became a "disorder." Sin visited the physician and became a "disease." Sin encountered the sociologist and became an "environmental response." Regardless of how we may redefine sin in our day, the fact remains: "All have sinned and fall short of the glory of God" (Romans 3:23). Then the Bible speaks and tells us that sin is both a state and an action. David said, "Surely I was sinful at birth" (Psalm 51:5). Furthermore, *sin* means "to miss the mark." Sin is unbelief (Romans 14:23), neglect of opportunity (James 4:17), transgression of God's law (1 John 3:4), and unrighteous acts (5:17).

C. The water symbolizes the Holy Spirit, who cleanses our hearts and delivers us from guilt so that we can live free from condemnation!

III. Sensitivity: "I Will Give You a New Heart and Spirit."

    A. Sin dulls our sensitivity to God. Ephesians 4:19 says, "Having lost all sensitivity, they have given themselves over to sensuality so as to indulge in every kind of impurity, with a continual lust for more." What a graphic portrait of our times.

    B. "I will put My Spirit within you and cause you to walk in My statutes" (Ezekiel 36:27, *NKJV*). God gives us the Holy Spirit to help us live a holy life (John 14:16, 17).

IV. Fellowship: "You Will Be My People."

When we sin against God we have the tendency to think that if we return to Him, we will be second-class citizens; something less than real sons and daughters; relegated to a servant status. There's a beautiful truth often overlooked in the parable of the prodigal son. The son says, "I'm no longer worthy to be called your son. Make me like one of your hired servants" (Luke 15:19, *NKJV*). But the father says, "My son who was lost is found, my son who was dead is alive" (see v. 24).

Illustration

Max Lucado tells the story of a woman named Maria and her daughter, Christina, who lived in a one-room house on the outskirts of a Brazilian village. Small as it was, they had done what they could to make a comfortable home.

Maria's husband had died when Christina was only a baby. A stubborn young woman, she refused opportunities to remarry and was determined to make the best life she could for herself and her baby. She got a job as a maid, which didn't pay much, but it enabled her to keep Christina with her while she worked. After 15 years had passed, the hardest years were over. Christina was now old enough to get a job and help out.

Christina was strong and independent like her mother. She resisted getting married at a young age, although she was very beautiful and had her opportunities to do so. She often spoke of going to the city. She dreamed of getting out of the village and experiencing the excitement of city life. The thought of this terrified her mother. Maria was always quick to remind Christina of the dangers of the city.

One morning her heart was broken as she awoke to find Christina's bed empty. She knew immediately where her daughter had gone. She put some clothes in a bag, gathered up all the money she had and headed for the city.

On her way to the bus stop, she went into a drugstore to get one last thing—photographs. She sat in the photograph booth, closed the curtain, and spent all she could having photographs made of herself. With her purse full of black-and-white photos, she boarded the next bus to Rio de Janeiro.

She knew that Christina had no way of earning money. She also knew that she was stubborn and would not give up. When pride meets hunger, people do things they would not ordinarily do. Knowing this, Maria began her search. Bars, hotels, nightclubs—any place with the reputation of streetwalkers or prostitutes. She went to them all, each time coming up empty. No one seemed to know Christina. But at each place, Maria left her photograph taped to a bathroom mirror, tacked to a hotel bulletin board, fastened to the corner of a phone booth. And on the back of each photo she wrote a note.

Before long, the money and the photos were gone, and Maria had to go back home. She sat down and wept uncontrollably as she arrived back home without her daughter.

A few weeks later young Christina walked down the hotel stairs. Her heart was broken; her innocence gone. The dream of city life had turned into her worst nightmare. She thought of their little home in the village. She wanted to go home. But could she? How could she ever face her mother after what she had done?

As she reached the bottom of the stairs, she stopped. She saw a familiar face. She looked again, and there on the lobby mirror was taped a black-and-white photograph of her mother. She couldn't believe her eyes. She walked across the room and took the small photo off the mirror. When she turned it over, she read this compelling invitation: "Whatever you have done, whatever you have become, it doesn't matter. Please come home." She did (Max Lucado, "Come Home," *Stories From the Heart*, p. 153).

Where Is Your God?

Text: Psalms 42; 43

One of the most painful emotions we experience in life is the feeling of loneliness. It has been estimated that some 70 percent of all Americans feel chronically lonely.

Loneliness does not mean to be alone. One can be in a crowd, yet feel very lonely. Loneliness is the feeling of being left out. It is the sense of being disconnected and cut off from others. It derives from a lack of belonging and a lack of intimacy with others. Loneliness results in an intense desire to be needed, to be included, to be wanted, to be loved, and to be accepted.

Three types of loneliness can be identified:

1. *Emotional loneliness* comes from the lack of close friendships. God said of Adam, "It is not good for the man to be alone" (Genesis 2:18). One-fourth of households consists of an individual living alone. Loneliness is a struggle for some single adults, divorcees, and for those whose spouse has died. It often derives from the lack of parental acceptance in childhood, lack of peer approval, and situations of loss such as the death of a spouse, divorce, retirement, or physical disability. Sometimes we can identify with the man who went to a psychiatrist and

requested the psychiatrist to give him a multiple personality. "Why do you want a multiple personality?" the psychiatrist asked. "At least I'd have someone to keep me company," was his reply.

2. *Social loneliness* is marked by feelings of aimlessness and marginal existence in the world. It comes from a lack of connection with one's peers or even society itself. It is caused by technology that overlooks people and depersonalizes society, extreme individualism that undermines community, hyper achievement that turns people into objects to be used for product and profit, appearance that values only the beautiful people, and mobility that affects family and community stability.

3. *Spiritual loneliness* comes from being estranged from God. The psalmist felt it when he asked "Where is God?" (see 42:3, 10). Jesus felt it on the cross: "My God, why have you forsaken me?" (Matthew 27:46; Mark 15:34).

   • We find ourselves at times asking with the psalmist, "Where is God?"
   • The doctor diagnoses us with a terminal disease, and we ask, "Where is God?"
   • Our prayers go unanswered, and we ask, "Where is God?"
   • Our children rebel against all we taught them, and we ask, "Where is God?"
   • The company downsizes and we are out of work, and we ask, "Where is God?"
   • Our ministry efforts produce little results, and we ask, "Where is God?"
   • We lose a loved one unexpectedly, and we ask, "Where is God?"

The psalmist gives the answer when he says, "Put your hope in God" (42:11; 43:5). He goes on in these psalms to resolve his loneliness in the presence of God. If the coming of the Holy Spirit means anything, if the baptism of the Spirit and the infilling of the Spirit mean anything, it means that in the midst of life's difficulties, we have a Comforter. And the presence of the Holy Spirit reassures us of the greatest promise found in the Bible: "I will never leave you nor forsake you" (Hebrews 13:5, *NKJV*).

Our emotions tell us God has left us, but faith tells us God is near. We need to learn to function out of our will, not our emotions. The psalmist makes three "I will" statements:

- I will praise Him (42:5, 11; 43:5).
- I will remember Him (42:6).
- I will go to the altar of God (43:4).

I.   I Will Praise Him (42:5, 11; 43:5).

We can respond to the difficulties of life with complaint, anger, hopelessness and fear, or with praise. Praise is an act of the will. Praise is based on two principles: who God is and what God has done (see Psalm 103:1-5).

When writer Anthony Burgess was 39, doctors found a brain tumor and gave him a year to live. He made a vow to write 10 novels in that last year so that his widow could live on the royalties. At the end of the year, he had completed five and a half novels, and the brain tumor had completely disappeared. He lived to age 76 and wrote about 50 novels and at least 15 nonfiction works. He was so prolific, even his publisher was unsure of the exact number of his books at the time of his death (*Speaker's Idea File*, August 1996, p. 2).

Illustration

II. I Will Remember Him (42:6).

A.   *The loneliness he feels.* The psalmist is exiled probably in Damascus of Syria during one of the invasions of the Arameans. He longs for the Promised Land. He thinks about the times he went to the Temple for the great festivals. He remembers the upper Jordan region and the Hermon Mountain Range with its peaks reaching 9,000 feet above sea level, and Mount Mizar, the water source of the Jordan River. The crashing waterfalls symbolize how overwhelmed he feels by his despair. Life is crashing down on him. Trouble after trouble falls on him until he feels as though he will be drowned.

B. *God tells us to remember.* We forget God's blessings. It's like small children. They want a gift or a new toy. Then they get it, and it doesn't take long for the new to wear off. They forget what was done for them as they focus their attention on a new toy. We, too, tend to forget God's salvation and His blessings. The newness of the new birth wears off. It becomes old hat. We lose the freshness, the vitality, and the joy of Christ's work in our hearts. "Forget not all his benefits" (103:2).

C. *The love he remembers.* Yet he remembers God's covenant love (42:8). This is the only reference to Yahweh in the psalm, which is the covenant name of God. Day after day he experiences God's care, protection and grace. God's love is the comfort to the soul beset by unanswered questions and depression. What we need to remember today is the love of God (Ephesians 3:18, 19). God is at work even in the most adverse circumstances.

Illustration

In the French Academy of Science, there is a rather plain, old shoemaker's awl on display. The story behind the awl is quite extraordinary. To look at it, one would never suspect that this simple tool could be responsible for anything of consequence. In fact, it caused tremendous pain. This was the awl that one day fell from the shoemaker's table and put out the eye of the shoemaker's 9-year-old son. The injury was so severe that the boy lost vision in both eyes and was enrolled in a special school for children who were blind. The boy learned to read by handling large, carved-wood blocks. When the shoemaker's son became an adult, he thought of a new way to read. It involved learning a system of dots translated into the letters of the alphabet that could be read from a piece of paper on any flat surface. Louis Braille actually used the awl which had blinded him as a boy to form the dots into a whole new reading system for the blind—known today as Braille.

III. I Will Go to the Altar of God (43:4).

A. The altar is the place where God dwells. The psalmist has in mind the brazen altar where the worshiper would bring an offering and invite those present to join him in praise to God. For us, it is a place of confession of sin, consecration of ourselves to God's will, and personal communion and fellowship with God.

B. Throughout Psalm 42, his longing for the presence of God is evident. He addresses him as "God," then as "the living God," and finally, describes his desire to see the "face of God" (see vv. 1-3).

Closing: We, too, need to go to the altar of God and meet Him face-to-face. There in His presence we will find fullness of joy and remember that we are never alone.

Simplicity!

Text: Luke 10:38-42

A TV commercial caught my attention. It opened with the scene of a downtown crowded street. There were bumper-to-bumper cars; a jackhammer was pounding. Construction workers were making street repairs; horns blaring. A taxicab driver was shouting at the car in front of him that was impeding his progress. Sidewalks were crowded with people pushing past each other to get to work on time. A pencil with an eraser appeared and began to erase each element of the scene. First the jackhammer, then the taxicab with its driver. As each character disappeared, so did its accompanying sound until only one car remained—the new model being advertised. Then the word SIMPLICITY appeared on the screen.

Simplicity is the cry of our age. Corporations are downsizing. More and more businessmen and businesswomen are fleeing the fast track of corporate life and moving beyond the suburbs to find a simpler, quieter lifestyle where they can spend more time at home and less time at the office. Even career politicians are resigning their long-held posts, tired of the hassles with the Washington pace and political heat.

But I thought of more than just the simplifying of our lifestyles as I watched that commercial; I reflected on the need for simplicity in our faith. Although Jesus talked about a childlike faith and told us that His yoke is easy and His burden light, we often find ourselves in a state of spiritual burnout, believing somehow that Jesus said, "Blessed are those who keep themselves busy, for theirs is the kingdom of heaven."

Have we lost the real simplicity of a relationship with God through Jesus? Has our religion become so cumbersome, legalistic, filled with a host of rules, regulations and rituals that we can no longer say, "The joy of the Lord is my strength?" No wonder Nietzche, the German agnostic, said that Christians would have to look more redeemed before he would believe their claims.

Jesus confronted the Pharisees and teachers of the Law about their complication of a spiritual life. They taught the traditions of men as the commandments of God (Matthew 15:8). They loved to parade around on the streets wearing their prayer shawls, but knew nothing of the secret prayer closet alone with God. They practiced minute details of their self-made legalistic rules, but they neglected the greater matters of justice, mercy and faithfulness (23:23). Jesus told them, "You strain out a gnat but swallow a camel" (v. 24).

When I read the Bible I am amazed at just how simple, and consequently joyful, true spirituality is (Ecclesiastes 12:11; Micah 6:8; Mark 12:30, 31; James 1:27). We need to come back to the simplicity of following Jesus. This was the case in the story of Jesus visiting the home of Martha and Mary. It speaks to me personally in profound ways, and I believe it holds some important truths for us all.

I.   We Need to Avoid Judging Each Other Spiritually.

Martha and Mary were different in their personalities and they exhibit a different spirituality. We don't need to judge each other spiritually (Matthew 7:1, 2). What is spirituality? David Benner says that *spirituality* is "the response to a deep and mysterious yearning for self-transcendence and surrender." Augustine prayed, "Our soul is restless until it finds rest in You, O Lord. For You made us for Yourself." Goethe observed, "All human longing is really the longing for God."

Christian spirituality is a deep, close and meaningful relationship with God made possible by the saving work of Jesus Christ and the indwelling of the Holy Spirit. Spiritual growth is merely growth in a relationship with God. Spirituality is different for different people.

A. *Head and heart.* Some people are more intellectual in their faith and enjoy in-depth Bible study and theology and ponder the mysteries of life, while others meet God in their hearts through emotions, experience and intuition.

B. *Discipline and spontaneity.* Some people follow set times for prayer, study and solitude, while others maintain a less rigorous style to their devotions, preferring rather to "pray without ceasing" (1 Thessalonians 5:17, *NKJV*).

C. *In the kitchen (Martha) and by the fireplace (Mary).* Martha invited Jesus to her home, but she had limited time for Him. Before we judge her too harshly, let's make sure we understand what Jesus said to her that day. Some have misconstrued the meaning of the passage, suggesting that Jesus was criticizing her organization, her hard work, her type A personality. He was not objecting to her preparing dinner. Without her cooking there would have been no dinner, including His, and He came by for dinner. He wanted to eat her good cooking like everyone else. I've heard some good Christians compare themselves to Martha in this story in a negative fashion and say, "I'm a Martha, not a Mary. I'm good with hospitality and service, but I'm not that good with spiritual matters like prayer, Bible teaching or counseling." But Jesus is not making light of Martha's strengths.

D. Balance is needed between set times for worship and just tuning in to God's presence throughout the day. We need to experience God in the midst of life. In his preface to *Grace Abounding*, John Bunyan asks, "Have you forgot . . . the milkhouse, the stable, the barn and the like, where God did visit your soul?"

II. Guard Against the Enemies of Joy.

    A. What, then, was Martha's problem? Jesus identified three issues that robbed her of spiritual simplicity:

        1. *She was distracted* (Greek, *perispao*: to draw away, to distract, to be over-preoccupied with something, to be cumbered). In 1 Corinthians 7:35 Paul uses the word in a negative form, *aperispastos*, to mean "undivided devotion to the Lord." Martha was trapped by the "tyranny of the urgent." She overdid things, and it robbed her of valuable time. She was preparing a seven-course meal when all Jesus wanted was soup and salad.

        2. *She was worried* (Greek, *merimnao*: to draw in different directions, to divide the mind). In Matthew 6:25, it is translated "take no thought" (KJV), that is, do not allow your mind to be conquered by anxious thoughts. Matthew 13:22 notes that the worries of this life choke the Word of God. Luke 21:34 states that the anxieties of life weigh our hearts down. *Worry* comes from an Anglo-Saxon word meaning "to choke."

        3. *She was upset about many things* (Greek, *thorubazo*: troubled). Paul uses this word in Acts 20:10, when he preached all night in Troas. About midnight, a young man named Eutychus fell out of a third-story window. Everyone thought he was dead. Paul threw himself over him and then told everyone, "Don't be alarmed . . . he's alive!" They went back upstairs, and he preached until daylight.

        4. *The example of Mary*: Jesus was not rewarding laziness. Mary was not a lazy person. She was, however, seizing a rare and unique opportunity to spend time with Jesus. In a world filled with the reality of worries, distractions and responsibilities, we would all do well to seize these rare, unique opportunities when they arise.

There are personal moments of inspiration when you feel the presence of God and hear His voice. There are special times in corporate worship when the Spirit of God visits a congregation in an unusual fashion.

B. When these times come, we need to tune in, sit at His feet, and give God our undivided attention. Mary did two important things that Jesus commended her for: She sat at His feet, and she listened to Him. Here is the posture of the true disciple of Jesus.

III. Remember, It's the Relationship That Counts.

God made us for a relationship. We know we're on track spiritually when our spirituality enhances our relationship to Jesus. We know we're getting off track when our spiritual activities diminish our sense of relationship with Him and put us on a treadmill of religious works, duties and laws. Only one religion speaks of God loving man and of man loving God—Christianity.

A. Adam and Eve walked with God in the cool of the day (Genesis 3:8).

B. Enoch walked with God (5:22-24).

C. Abraham was called the friend of God (2 Chronicles 20:7).

D. Moses spoke with God face-to-face as a man speaks to his friend (Exodus 33:11).

E. David was called a man after God's heart (1 Samuel 13:14).

F. Jesus said, "I call you friends" (John 15:15) and taught us to pray, "Our Father" (Matthew 6:9).

G. Paul said, "I want to know Christ" (Philippians 3:10). *The Amplified Bible* puts it this way: "[For my determined purpose is] that I may know Him [that I may progressively become more deeply and intimately acquainted with Him, perceiving and recognizing and understanding the wonders of His Person more strongly and more clearly]."

IV. Jesus Goes Where He Is Invited.

    A. Martha opened her home to Him. What a beautiful picture of salvation—welcoming Him who knocks on the door of our hearts (Revelation 3:20). Jesus does not force His way in. That day, Jesus initiated the contact when He came to their village of Bethany. But Martha had to invite Him to her home, and we have to invite Him into our hearts to be saved.

    B. The issue is not, does He want us, but do we want Him? You may say, "I have nothing to bring to Him, nothing to give Him for His service." Give Him yourself. He's not looking for the most talented, the most gifted, the most resourceful, but those who are willing and obedient.

It's for Sinners. The noted Scottish theologian, John Duncan of New College in Edinburgh, was attending a service held in a Church of Scotland on one occasion. As Communion was being served, he noticed that a young girl of about 20 turned her head away as the elements came to her. She motioned for the elder who was serving to take the cup away because she couldn't drink it. Realizing what was going on, he reached his hand over, touched her shoulder and said, "Take it, sweetheart, it's for sinners" (Graham, *Born Again*, p. 115).

Illustration

Sowing and Reaping

Text: Galatians 6:7-9

W hen God created the universe, He established laws to govern it. These laws govern everything from atoms to attitudes, radar to relationships, protons to people.

A *law* is simply "a rule or principle which brings about a certain result when obeyed." Laws are fixed, absolute and predictable. Laws give our world order, design and balance.

Not only does the natural world operate by the laws of God, so does the spiritual world. God spoke from Mount Sinai and gave the Ten Commandments, which we call the Law of God. Ours is a nation of laws which secure our safety, protection and prosperity. The entire Bible is referred to as the Law of God (Psalm 1:2; James 1:25).

One of the most important spiritual laws is the law of sowing and reaping: "Do not be deceived . . ." (Galatians 6:7-9). Paul reiterates this law to the Corinthians: "Remember this: Whoever sows sparingly will also reap sparingly, and whoever sows generously will also reap generously" (2 Corinthians 9:6).

I.   We Reap What We Sow.

This sounds simple enough, but let's consider the implications of this truth. A basic law of physics states that for every action there is an equal and opposite reaction.

A. We get out of life what we put into it. This does not mean that we directly cause every event in our lives; we do not. For example, when Jesus was about to heal the blind man, the disciples asked, "Who sinned, this man or his parents?" (Matthew 9:2). Jesus said, "Neither" (v. 3). In other words, all human suffering is not the direct result of someone's sin. However, all suffering is the indirect result of Adam's sin (Romans 5:12). This illustrates the law of sowing and reaping.

B. In many areas of our lives, we must own up to the fact that we get out of life what we put into life. Life is a series of investments and returns. Remember, every action produces an equal and opposite reaction. If we sow, we will reap.

1. Give money—receive blessings
2. Invest money—accumulate savings
3. Borrow money—incur debt
4. Venture nothing—gain nothing
5. Live honorably—receive honor
6. Study diligently—achieve an education
7. Train for athletic competition—win the prize
8. Show kindness—kindness is shown in return

Illustration

Sow a thought—reap a word
Sow a word—reap an action
Sow an action—reap a habit
Sow a habit—reap a character
Sow a character—reap a destiny

II. We Reap the Same Kind That We Sow.

Jesus points this out: "By their fruit you will recognize them. Do people pick grapes from thornbushes, or figs from thistles? Likewise every good tree bears good fruit, but a bad tree bears bad fruit" (Matthew 7:16, 17).

A. The point is simple, but it must be clearly stated: We cannot plant corn and get a harvest of wheat; we cannot plant tomatoes and get a harvest of cucumbers. Neither can we plant seeds of criticism, strife and anger and get a healthy marriage. We cannot plant seeds of stinginess, self-indulgence, and greed and reap a harvest of financial blessing. We cannot plant seeds of poor decisions and reap a harvest of God's will in our lives. We reap the same kind that we sow.

B. There are two types of harvests:

   1. *The flesh.* The Greek word Paul uses is *sarx*—the sin nature; the nature of man devoid of the Spirit of God. In Freudian terms, it is the *id* that seeks to avoid pain, relieve tension, and obtain pleasure—biological, instinctual urges that seek expression regardless of social or divine boundaries. I read that some people sow wild oats six days a week and come to church on Sunday and pray for a crop failure!

      a. Job 4:8 says, "As I have observed, those who plow evil and those who sow trouble reap it."

      b. Proverbs 22:8 says, "He who sows wickedness reaps trouble, and the rod of his fury will be destroyed."

      c. Hosea 8:7 says, "They sow the wind and reap the whirlwind."

   2. *The Spirit.* Sow to the desires and dictates of the Holy Spirit in your life (Galatians 5:16, 17). The result? "The fruit of the Spirit is love, joy, peace, patience, kindness, goodness, faithfulness, gentleness and self-control" (vv. 22, 23). How do we do that? By filling our minds and hearts with the Word, prayer, fellowship, obeying God when He speaks, and by guarding our hearts and minds from the influences of the world.

III. We Reap in Proportion to What We Sow.

If you've ever planted any kind of fruit or vegetables, you understand this truth. What a large harvest can come from a small amount of seeds (Luke 6:38). Here are two areas of life that illustrate the concept:

A. *Relationships.* Notice the impact of a kind word or a compliment versus a harsh word or criticism. The friendlier we are, the friendlier the world becomes. The more positive we are, the more positive others are toward us. Jesus said, "Do to others as you would have them do to you" (v. 31).

B. *Giving.* God stresses this promise throughout Scripture. "Sow generously," Paul reminds us (see 2 Corinthians 9:6). Listen to the Old Testament prophet in Malachi 3:7-10.

Illustration

A missionary from Chile told of a pastor from an extremely poor village who was confronted by the Holy Spirit that he was not teaching the people all God's truth. He failed to teach them about tithing. "But these people are so poor," he argued with God, "they have nothing to give." "Teach them anyway," the Lord seemed to press upon his heart. So the pastor did. He slowly took them through the Scripture explaining God's plan of tithing. The next Sunday, the people arrived with their tithe—chickens, fruits, vegetables, eggs, leather goods and all kinds of handmade articles. The pastor sold some of the goods and used the money for the work of the church. He gave some of the gifts to the destitute in the village and kept some for his own livelihood. Sunday after Sunday the people gave. A severe drought swept through the area. But, miraculously, the crops of the church members continued to flourish. Their fields were green and lush, while those in surrounding areas withered. Relative abundance replaced abject poverty. They began selling their crops, and their tithes included money. They were able to build a meeting place for their congregation. The point is, the law of sowing and reaping works regardless of the circumstances (Robertson, *The Secret Kingdom,* pp. 109-111).

IV. We Reap in a Different Season Than We Sow.

Paul reminds us that we reap "at the proper time" (Galatians 6:9) or "in due season" (KJV). This contains both a promise (positive effects) and a caution (negative effects).

A. *Promise.* Parenting is an excellent illustration. Proverbs 22:6 reminds us that if we train our children right, when they are old, they will not depart from it. It has been said that raising children is about as easy as nailing a poached egg to a tree. Parenting involves making a long-term investment in our children. Many times we get frustrated as parents because we do not see the immediate payoff of our investment with our children. We forget that everything we learned in our lives came "through many dangers, toils and snares," and so we expect our children to learn every lesson in life from us, to heed our counsel, and to not make the same mistakes we made.

B. *Caution.* I remember when boxer Tommy Morrison announced he was HIV positive. I listened to his testimony at a press conference as he spoke of the promiscuous lifestyle he lived in the past. He said, "I never thought I was at risk. It could never happen to me." He went on to say, "I've jeopardized my family and the rest of my life." Then he looked straight into the TV camera and said, "Think about that."

C. *Expectation.* We must learn to wait on God's proper season for our lives. God's timing is perfect. It's not always according to our schedule or desire. But the promise is sure—we will reap in due time!

V. We Reap If We Persevere.

"If we do not give up" (v. 9). The perseverance principle is taught in Scripture over and over (Matthew 24:13; Luke 18:1; Hebrews 12:1).

Churchill: Never Give In! Churchill was invited to deliver the commencement address at his alma mater, Harrow School. The auditorium was hot and the program tedious. When introduced, he approached the podium and delivered a 29-word speech: "Never give in, never give in, never, never, never, never. In nothing great or small, large or petty, never give in, except to convictions of honor and good sense."

Illustration

First Things First

New Year's Message

Text: Matthew 6:33

One of the most important lessons for life involves setting and maintaining priorities—putting first things first.

Without priorities . . .

- The athlete fails to win the prize
- Couples fail to achieve marital happiness
- Financial goals go unmet
- Businesses go bankrupt
- Churches become stagnant in their ministries
- Students fail to make the grade
- Dreams remain unfulfilled
- Parents falter in raising their children properly.

Jesus stressed the importance of priorities to His disciples when He said, "But seek first the kingdom of God and His righteousness, and all these things shall be added to you" (Matthew 6:33, *NKJV*). Christ makes this challenge while delivering what we call the Sermon on the Mount (Matthew 5–7). The teaching outlines the distinctive lifestyle of His followers who, through faith in Him, had entered the kingdom of God. Matthew 5:1 reminds us that He was not merely addressing a crowd of indifferent onlookers or miracle seekers, but His "disciples," those who had made a commitment to Him.

We need to understand the spiritual context in which He made the challenge. He had just told them several important truths:

1. "Do not lay up for yourselves treasures on earth . . . but . . . treasures in heaven" (6:19, 20, *NKJV*).
2. "For where your treasure is, there your heart will be also" (v. 21).
3. "No one can serve two masters. . . . You cannot serve both God and Money" (v. 24).
4. "Do not worry . . ." (vv. 25-32). Then He explains that the only way we can lay up treasures in heaven, serve God and not Money, and conquer worry is to "seek first the kingdom of God and His righteousness" (v. 33, *NKJV*).

Sounds promising, especially that part about "all these things will be given to you as well." But what does it mean to seek first the Kingdom? Jesus tells us that the thread which runs throughout every priority in our lives is the kingdom of God. So the essential question of the disciple is, Does every area of my life serve the interests of the kingdom of God, or my own interests? If putting first things first is so important, then we must decide exactly what comes first—in a word, *the Kingdom*.

What is the Kingdom? The Greek word *baselia* means "the rule of God; the sphere of God's rule; located wherever the king rules." E.S. Jones said, "The kingdom of God is God's total answer for man's total need." In the New Testament the term *kingdom of heaven* (used 33 times) and *kingdom of God* (used 67 times) are synonymous.

Jesus awakened hope in His day with the announcement: "Repent, for the kingdom of heaven is near" (4:17). What was so unique about Jesus' announcement? He proclaimed that the Kingdom was here and now, not in the future. Not only did He announce the Kingdom, He demonstrated the Kingdom through signs, miracles and wonders. He opened the doors of the Kingdom to "whosoever will" enter, regardless of race, creed, gender or status. His kingdom is established in the hearts of everyone who

believes in Him as Savior and Lord. The only pr
entrance is not legalistic righteousness, keeping the
al knowledge but, rather, being born-again (John 3:3-17).

Now that we are in the Kingdom, and King Jesus Christ reigns
as Lord, how can we seek this Kingdom?

I. Prioritize Your Relationship to God Over All Other Relationships.

To seek the Kingdom begins with seeking the King. The
Kingdom cannot be separated from the King himself. All other
relationships fall into place when our relationship with Christ
is in place. Remember the greatest commandment—to love
God—then we are prepared to love our neighbors. My relationship with my wife, my children, my congregation, and others are healthy when my relationship with Christ is first.

A. Do you find yourself in an unproductive relationship? Are
you codependent? Learn to depend on Christ. Are you in
a controlling relationship? Then submit to Christ. Are you
easily manipulated by others? Then experience freedom
in Christ. Are you easily rejected? Then rest in the unconditional love of Christ.

B. Seeking God means to pursue, chase after, long for, and
desire. Spiritual growth does not come to the complacent
but to those who seek. God says, "You will seek me and
find me when you seek me with all your heart" (Jeremiah
29:13). We need to be diligent about our spiritual growth.

II. Prioritize Eternal Investments Over Temporary Ones.

The Kingdom is an eternal Kingdom. The statement connects
with Matthew 6:19-21, where Jesus tells us to lay up for ourselves "treasures in heaven." He deals with the struggle all disciples experience in dealing with living in a dual universe. The
world in which we live is both spiritual and material, eternal and
earthly. We must learn to balance these two realities. When we
think about investments we need to think about the heavenly as
well as the earthly. Tithing, serving, and missions work are

investments in the Kingdom. Spending time with your family is more important than making a little more money. The money won't mean anything if you don't have a family to enjoy.

While the *Titanic* was sinking into the freezing, raging waters of the North Atlantic, a frightened woman in a lifeboat about to be lowered into the water suddenly remembered something she needed that was in her room. She asked permission to go back to her room. She was given three minutes, or they would leave without her. She ran across the deck that was already slanted at a dangerous angle. She raced through the gambling room with all the money rolled to one side, ankle deep. She came to her stateroom and quickly pushed aside her diamond rings, bracelets and necklaces as she reached to the shelf above her bed and grabbed three small oranges. She rushed back to the lifeboat and got in. What is incredible about the event is that 30 minutes earlier, before the ship hit an iceberg, she would not have chosen three oranges over her priceless jewelry. But death had boarded the *Titanic* and transformed all sense of values. The priceless became worthless, and the worthless became priceless. When Christ enters our hearts and sets up His kingly rule, all values are transformed.

Illustration

III. Prioritize Who You Are Over What You Do.

Focus on character development rather than achievement and accomplishment. Righteousness is the quality of the Kingdom.

A. *Righteousness and peace.* The prophets described the character of the Kingdom as one of righteousness and peace (Isaiah 9:6, 7).

B. *True righteousness.* The entire Sermon on the Mount deals with the subject of true versus false righteousness (Matthew 5:20). The righteousness that exceeds that of the Pharisees (pious or pure ones) is the righteousness that comes as a gift from God and is received by faith (Genesis 15:6; Philippians 3:7-9). The difference between Jesus and the Pharisees concerned the Law. While the Old Testament never teaches obedience to the Law as the means for salvation, the Pharisees developed this idea before the time of Jesus during the intertestamental period (280 B.C. until Christ). Jesus taught the unconditional love for all people and salvation as a free gift (John 3:16). They focused on the interpretation of the Law, while Jesus stressed the intent of the Law. Thus, He says, "In everything, do to others what you would have them do to you, for this sums up the Law and the Prophets" (Matthew 7:12).

C. *Two sides of righteousness.* We are in a justified position before God in Christ, but we must then practice righteousness, which means doing the will of God. Christ outlines righteous living in the Beatitudes (5:3-12).

At a young age, John C. Rockefeller Sr. demonstrated strength and determination in his goals. By age 33 he earned his first million dollars. By 43 he controlled the largest company in the world, and at 53 was the richest man in the world and the world's only billionaire. He then developed a strange disease (alopecia) where his hair fell out, his eyebrows and eyelashes disappeared, and he was shrunken like a mummy. While his weekly income was $1 million, his diet consisted of milk and crackers. He was so hated in Pennsylvania that he maintained bodyguards. He could not sleep, and all joy for living left him. The medical diagnosis predicted he would not live another year. The newspaper wrote his obituary in advance. During those sleepless nights, he began to take stock of himself. He realized he could not take any of his money with him. One morning he awoke with new resolve. He began helping churches and charities with his money and feeding the poor and needy. He established the Rockefeller Foundation, whose funding led to the discovery of penicillin and other wonder drugs. He began to sleep again. Joy filled his heart. The symptoms began to disappear. Instead of dying at 54 as predicted, he lived to be 98.

Illustration

Closing: Kingdom priorities bring great blessings: "All these things will be given to you as well."

The Winning Spirit

Text: Numbers 13; 14; Joshua 6; 14

Winston Churchill once said, "Success is going from one failure to another without losing your enthusiasm." Regardless of who we are, we desire to be successful in life. I have never met a person who actually set out to be a failure at any endeavor.

There are those who feel as though success will never be theirs. They envision themselves as being too inadequate for the challenge, or lacking the necessary resources, or facing too many obstacles to ever reach their goals. As a result, they stop dreaming. They learn to live with the status quo. Some people identify with the man who said, "I've come to the conclusion that the key to success just doesn't fit my ignition."

What we need is a role model—an example of faith who can show us the way, not a man born with a silver spoon in his mouth. He is one who had to achieve success "through many dangers, toils and snares." That man is an Old Testament personality named Caleb. The Bible gives us very little background of Caleb. We know that he was from the tribe of Judah, the son of Jephunneh (Numbers 13:6). He was one of the 12 spies Moses chose to spy out the Land of Promise. The group spied out the land for 40 days and then returned to the camp of the Israelites at Kadesh in the Desert of Paran (v. 26).

Everything was going as planned. The spies reported: The land is flowing with milk and honey. They brought back some of its luscious fruit. The people began to get excited about their new home until one of the spies said the word that brings all dreams to a grinding halt: *But!*

- *But* the people are powerful.
- *But* the cities are fortified.
- *But* there are giants in the land!

Then Caleb, along with Joshua, silenced the people and said, "We should go up and take possession of the land, for we can certainly do it" (v. 30). But the other spies spread a bad report among the people. "We can't do it," they said. And added, "We are like grasshoppers before them" (see vv. 31-33). The people grumbled against the Lord and against Moses and Aaron. "Why is the Lord bringing us to this land only to let us fall by the sword?" they asked. "We should choose a leader and go back to Egypt" (14:3, 4).

Then God spoke. The result was that a generation was forbidden to enter the Promised Land. Because of their faithlessness and disobedience, they would spend the next 40 years in the desert. But God gave a promise: Two men and their families would enter the land after the wilderness experience was complete—Joshua and Caleb. God made a remarkable statement about Caleb: "But because my servant Caleb has a different spirit and follows me wholeheartedly, I will bring him into the land" (v. 24).

What we need for success in life is the "Caleb spirit." He had the spirit of a winner. Caleb resolved to conquer all obstacles in his goal of possessing the promises of God. He gives us four lessons for life:

I. Caleb Silenced the Opposition (Numbers 13:30).

A. Everyone faces opposition to their dreams and goals through criticism, adversity and unbelief. We have to silence the opposition in order to succeed.

B. Joshua remembered this principle 40 years later when they invaded Jericho. He didn't allow the people to speak when they marched around Jericho (Joshua 6). Joshua knew that if he allowed them to speak as they marched around Jericho, they would begin to speak words of unbelief. I can hear them now: "Look at the size of the walls. What if they begin to shoot down arrows at us and cast huge stones? They will crush us like ants! What kind of strategy is this, marching around this fortified city? We're sitting ducks out here!" They would have talked themselves out of victory and never made it to the seventh day if they had spoken words of doubt. So Joshua only allowed them to speak on the seventh day. "Shout! For the Lord has given you the city!" (v. 16).

President Theodore Roosevelt put opposition into perspective in his address at the Sorbonne, Paris, France, April 23, 1910:

Illustration

It is not the critic who counts: not the man who points out how the strong man stumbled or where the doer of deeds could have done them better. The credit belongs to the man who is actually in the arena; whose face is marred by dust and sweat and blood; who strives valiantly; who errs, and comes short again and again, because there is not effort without error and shortcoming; who actually tries to do the deed; who knows the great enthusiasm, the great devotion, and spends himself in a worthy cause; who, at the worst, if he fails, at least fails while daring greatly.

Far better it is to dare mighty things, to win glorious triumphs even though checkered by failure than to rank with these poor spirits who neither enjoy nor suffer much because they live in the gray twilight that knows neither victory nor defeat.

II. Caleb Advanced the Kingdom of God (Numbers 14:6-9).

A. We have but two options in life: advance or retreat. It's been said if you're not actively pursuing the person you want to be, you are pursuing the person you don't want to be. Status quo is a prelude to retreat and regression.

B. Israel responded to the presence of giants in the land by retreating. "Let's go back to Egypt." Egypt is easy . . . comfortable . . . without challenges . . . demands no faith.

C. I guess they forgot what it was like to be in slavery. Or maybe they had gotten conditioned to being slaves and didn't know how to live in liberty. Egypt is less than God's best, affords us no opportunities, and keeps us in a subservient role. We should never be content in Egypt. We need to get out of our own Egyptian bondages and move on to the Promised Land of abundant living that God has ordained for us! We, like Israel at the Red Sea, need to "move on" (Exodus 14:15).

Illustration

Dan Janzen, the speed skater, was one of the hard-luck stories of the 1988 Winter Olympics. He faced an even greater disappointment in 1992. But instead, he turned failure into success. During the 1988 games, Dan's sister was dying of cancer. Consequently, he was unable to concentrate on the race. Even though he was a gold-medal favorite, he failed miserably. First, he fell during the 500-meter race on Valentine's Day. Four days later, he fell again in the 1,000-meter.

In 1992 he had a chance to redeem himself. But once again, he started the 500-meter with a burst of power but fell on the ice. Only the grueling 1,000-meter race lay before him—his last opportunity to win. Could he overcome fear and anxiety? Only one person in the stadium at Lillehammer knew whether or not he could do it—Dan Janzen. For days he had been telling himself, "I like the 1,000."

When the gun sounded, he started off at a world-record pace. Lap after lap, he skated with strength and confidence. Then, on the next to the last turn, he brushed his hand on the ice and it looked as if he would fall again. But this time, he kept his balance. Seconds later, he crossed the finish line with his arms raised in victory. Not only had he won the gold, he had set a new world record for the 1,000.

III. Caleb Waited for the Promise of God (Joshua 14:6-8).

    A. The unbelief of others cost Caleb 40 years in the wilderness. Whether we like it or not, the responses and actions of others sometimes affect us negatively.

    B. You may be suffering a setback today in your own life because of the irresponsibility of others.

    C. How did Caleb respond? Did he get angry at God? After all, he believed God. He could have said, "God, this isn't fair. How can You allow me to suffer and to miss out on Your promises because of the faithlessness of others?" He could have become bitter toward those who placed the whole community in a desert for 40 years. But he didn't.

        1. He persevered in his faith and waited for the promises of God to be fulfilled in his own life.

        2. He maintained his convictions in the promises of God when others failed to believe.

        3. What a witness. You may have to do the same on your job, in your home, at your school.

Illustration

An article appeared in the *Atlanta Journal-Constitution* (April 10, 1996, A12) titled "Stand Up for Faith, Scalia Says." The article reported the recent speech delivered by Supreme Court Justice Antonin Scalia to an event sponsored by the Christian Legal Society at the Mississippi College School of Law. He said that Christians must proclaim their belief in miracles and ignore the scorn of the "worldly wise." He went on to say that the modern world dismisses Christians as fools for holding to their traditional beliefs. "We are fools for Christ," he said. "We must pray for the courage to endure the scorn of the sophisticated world."

IV. Caleb Was Willing to Fight for What He Wanted (Joshua 14:10-14).

    A. The gift of faith is free, but the life of faith is a fight. You have to fight for your goals, your family, your career, your ministry. His resolve to win was based on his confidence in God: "The Lord helping me, I will drive them out just as he said" (v. 12).

B. He made a powerful affirmation we need to learn to make, "Give me this mountain!" (*NKJV*). He was 85 years old when he made this affirmation. He was ready and willing to claim his inheritance no matter how long he had to wait to receive it.

C. Go forth and claim your inheritance. Lay claim to God's promises. Fight whatever spiritual battles you need to fight to achieve victory. Don't stop short of the promises. And don't let the unbelief of others discourage you and keep you from your inheritance.

Rise and Be Healed

Text: Matthew 9:1-8

When we read the Bible, we come face-to-face with the God of healing. There are 30 recorded cases of healing in the Old Testament and 38 in the New Testament. One-fifth of the Gospels deals with Christ's healing ministry. The word *heal* means "to save, mend, restore, cure, soothe and cleanse."

When the Israelites came out of Egypt and prepared for the desert, God spoke to them: "I am the Lord, who heals you" (Exodus 15:26). God revealed Himself through the covenant name *Jehovah Rapha*, "the Lord your Healer."

There are powerful promises and principles of healing in both Testaments (Psalm 103:3; 107:20; Proverbs 3:7, 8; Malachi 4:2; Matthew 4:23; 8:17; 14:14; Luke 4:18; Acts 10:38; 1 Corinthians 12:7-11; James 5:16).

When we mention healing, a number of questions are raised:

- Is it always God's will to heal?
- Is healing for today, or did it cease with the apostolic church?
- Why isn't everyone healed?
- Why do we anoint the sick with oil?
- Are the elders the only ones who can pray for the sick?

One of the early incidences of Christ's healing was that of a cripple who was brought to Jesus on a mat. They tore off the roof of a house where Jesus was teaching in their resolution to get their friend to Jesus. We need to remember first that healings and miracles are different. Sometimes healing is a form of a miracle, so there is an instantaneous result. But the word *healing* means "a process of recovery." To pray for healing, then, is to ask God for recovery power for some injury to the body, the mind or the spirit. People get disappointed when all their symptoms don't instantly disappear when they pray because they don't understand that healing takes time. God may require us to do something for healing to be complete. Prayer is not the only thing needed for healing. Often it has to be followed up with action steps of diet, exercise and treatment. Every person praying for healing needs to remember that we should never pray a prayer of which we are not willing to be part of the answer.

Now what do we learn from this account of healing?

I. **Healing Takes Place in an Atmosphere of Faith and Love.**
   "When Jesus saw their faith . . ." (Matthew 9:2). These men cared about their friend. Here we see a model for the church. "Faith expresses itself through love" (see Galatians 5:6). The church is commissioned as a healing community, the body of Christ on the earth. Our essential ministry is healing—spirit, mind and body. Here are atmospheric conditions needed for the church to be a healing community:
   A. *Unconditional love* (John 13:34, 35)
   B. *Unity of spiritual purpose* (Acts 4:32)
   C. *Unconditional acceptance* (Romans 15:7). Revelation 22:17 says, "The Spirit and the bride say, 'Come!' And let him who hears say, 'Come!' Whoever is thirsty, let him come; and whoever wishes, let him take the free gift of the water of life."
   D. *Compassionate involvement* (Galatians 6:2; Romans 15:1). The laying on of hands is a symbol of our involvement with human suffering. Jesus himself touched the leper.

E. *Expectant faith.* Jesus saw the faith of those who helped their friend that day. The physical body itself responds positively to attitudes of faith and hope.

> *To live above with saints we love,*
> *Oh that will be glory.*
> *To live below with saints we know,*
> *now that's a different story.*

Illustration

II. Healing Works From the Inside Out.

Jesus told the paralytic, "Be of good cheer, your sins are for-given" (Matthew 9:2). It is interesting that Jesus doesn't immediately heal him of his paralysis. Instead He says, "Son, be of good cheer, your sins are forgiven." Here we see inner healing—the healing of the soul (Psalm 23:3; 41:4). What is the greatest healing? Is it not the healing of the soul?

A. *The healing of the soul.* There are four types of pain:
   1. *Hurt* (rejection, disappointment)
   2. *Humiliation* (put-downs, criticisms)
   3. *Horror* (fears)
   4. *Hate* (unforgiveness, resentment)

B. *The danger of repression.* We bury our pain in the uncon-scious through denial, rationalization and projection. This causes psychosomatic illnesses.

C. *The inner healing work of the Holy Spirit.* This comes through confrontation and confession (James 5:16).

In the *Lexington Herald-Leader* (9/23/84), an article appeared from the *New York Times* News Service titled "Confession May Be Good for the Body." It read: "Confession, whatever it may do for the soul, appears to be good for the body. New studies show per-suasively that people who are able to confide in others about their troubled feelings or some traumatic event, rather than bear the tur-moil in silence, are less vulnerable to disease." The article includ-ed several experiments that confirm the "long-term health bene-fits" of sharing our pain with others. Dr. James Pennebaker, of

Illustration

Johns Hopkins School of Medicine, conducted research that shows "the act of confiding in someone else protects the body against damaging internal stresses that are the penalty for carrying around an onerous emotional burden such as unspoken remorse." Similar research conducted at Harvard University shows that those who do not share have "less effective immune systems."

Do you remember Jesus' conversation with the woman at the well? She tried to avoid any confrontation until He said, "Go, call your husband." She responded, "I don't have a husband." To which He said, "I know. You've had five husbands, and the man you are living with now is not your husband." Shocked, she said, "I perceive that you are a prophet." But that began her healing because He loved her in spite of her past. She ran into the village proclaiming, "I have met the Messiah, and He told me everything I ever did." She did not mean that He had simply read her mail, but that she could be completely open to Him about her painful past, and He loved her still (see John 4:4-42).

Illustration

III. Healing Often Involves a Plan of Action.

Jesus told the paralytic, "Get up, take your mat and go home" (Matthew 9:6). We need to put our faith in action. "Faith . . . if it is not accompanied by action, is dead [useless, lifeless]" (James 2:17). We have to follow up on our prayers with action.

A. Moses put in the branch to heal the bitter waters of Marah (Exodus 15:23-25).

B. Elisha told Naaman to dip in the Jordan seven times (2 Kings 5:10).

C. Jesus told the lepers to go and show themselves to the priest (Luke 17:14).

D. The woman with the issue of blood touched the hem of His garment (8:43, 44).

E. Peter and John took the cripple by the hand and said, "In the name of Jesus, rise and walk" (Acts 3:6, 7).

Conformed or Transformed?

Text: Romans 12:2

Michelangelo described the art of sculpture as the making of men. He said that his role was to simply free men and women from the prison of stone. Instead of trying to fashion the image of a man from stone, he chiseled away the excess stone which kept the image hidden. He had the ability to look at a piece of marble and envision the great works of *David*, the *Pieta*, *Moses* and the *Bacchus*.

In a very real way, this illustrates the primary work of the Holy Spirit in human experience— the making of men and women in the image of Christ. Originally, we were created in the image of God (Genesis 1:26). Sin marred the image. Christ came to redeem us from our sins and restore us in His image and likeness. The Holy Spirit lives in the believer's heart, transforming him or her from glory to glory (see Romans 8:29, 30; 2 Corinthians 3:18; Ephesians 4:22-24; Colossians 3:10).

There were times when, out of frustration, Michelangelo quit working on a sculpture—as in the case of the statue of *Saint*

Matthew, which he left half finished. He said the stone refused to release the prisoner. He left several unfinished, four of the most magnificent being the *Captive Giants* in Florence.

Not so with the Holy Spirit. He will finish what He started in us. A man once asked Rembrandt at what point a painting is complete. He responded, "A painting is finished when it expresses the intent of the artist." The most reassuring verse for every believer is Philippians 1:6. Jesus is both the Author and the Finisher of our faith (Hebrews 12:2)!

Suddenly we gain a new insight into the power of worship. Worship facilitates this transformation process of Christlikeness. This is what Paul has in mind in Romans 12:1, 2. He connects spiritual worship with the transformation of our lives. We become what we worship.

- If we worship money, we become materialists.
- If we worship pleasure, we become hedonists.
- If we worship power, we control and manipulate others for our own ends.
- If we worship fame, we become gods in our own eyes.
- If we worship our abilities, we become humanists.
- If we worship intellect, we become atheists.
- If we worship the self, we become narcissists.

However, when we worship God in spirit and in truth, as Jesus said we should, we are transformed into God's true likeness, so that men see Christ in us, the hope of glory!

Illustration

A little girl in my congregation handed me a note she wrote with a crayon one day after the service. It read: "Why did God create Adam before He created Eve? Everyone knows you make a rough draft before you create a masterpiece!"

I.   Be Not Conformed to the Pattern of This World.

A.   *From decision to dedication.* Paul's primary concern here is that we follow up on our decision for Christ with a dedication to Him. The living sacrifice needs to be bound with cords to the horns of the altar (Psalm 118:27). Also, the verb shifts from the aorist tense, *offer your bodies*, to the present tense, indicating the necessity for continued vigilance lest our decision grow weak. The threat to dedicated living is the world.

B. *Conformed*, or *fashioned*, is *suschematizesthai*, the root of which is *schema,* which means "the outward form varies from day to day, or season to season." A person's *schema,* or shape, varies from 7 to 17 to 70. It refers to the outward shape or image of something that can be changed and speaks of that which is transitory, changeable and unstable. In this context it means to be shaped by external pressures, styles or allurements. Hence, *Phillips* translates it, "Don't let the world around you squeeze you into its own mold" (Romans 12:2). Paul is saying, "Don't try to match your life to all the fashions of this world; don't be like a chameleon, which takes its color from its surroundings" (Barclay).

Robert Frost, in his poem "The Road Not Taken," says:
Two roads diverged in a wood, and I—
I took the one less traveled by,
And that has made all the difference.

Illustration

II. Be Transformed.

Here's the good news—if you don't like the person you are (and I'm sure most of us have some things we don't like about ourselves), we can change by the grace of God!

A. The word *transformed* (*metamorphoo*) means "to change into another form." It comes from *meta* (change) and *morpho* (form). The only other uses of the word in the New Testament are in Matthew 17:2, for the Transfiguration of Christ, and 2 Corinthians 3:18, where Paul describes the transformation of believers into the image of Christ in all His moral and spiritual excellencies. *Morpho* refers to inner change that is lasting and permanent. It describes the essential unchanging shape or essence of anything. True worship results in the ongoing change of the true person, the inward personality. God wants us to have real change in our nature and personality, not just surface change that is an exterior image.

B. The process of transformation is the renewing of your mind. The way we think determines the way we live. Emerson said, "A man is what he thinks about all day long." The word for *renew* is *anakainosis*, from *kainos*, which means "new in point of character and nature" as opposed to new in time (*neos*). When a person is in Christ, he or she is *kainos,* new in nature and character. His mind is different, for the mind of Christ is in him (1 Corinthians 2:16; Philippians 2:5).

C. The goal of transformation is to put into practice the will of God. Right thinking results in right living. "As he thinks in his heart, so is he" (Proverbs 23:7, *NKJV*). The will of God speaks of a relationship of intimacy with Him by which we are changed into His image.

Illustration

Betty Wein retells an old tale she heard from Elie Wiesel. A just man comes to Sodom hoping to save the city. He pickets. What else can he do? He goes from street to street, from marketplace to marketplace, shouting, "Men and women, repent. What you are doing is wrong. It will kill you; it will destroy you."

They laugh, but he goes on shouting, until one day a child stops him.

"Poor stranger, don't you see it's useless?"

"Yes," the man replies.

"Then why do you go on?" the child asks.

"At first I was convinced that I would change them. Now I go on shouting because I don't want them to change me" (Craig B. Larson, editor, *Illustrations for Preaching & Teaching*, p. 109).

No Excuse

Text: Romans 1:18-20

William Glasser, in his book *Reality Therapy,* makes the statement that "man is not irresponsible because he is ill; he is ill because he is irresponsible." Our age has been marked the age of victimization. Victimization cries, "It's not my fault!" Victimization blames other people and circumstances for one's predicament, blocks the pathway to personal responsibility, and engages in endless self-pitying. Today we have no-fault automobile insurance, no-fault divorces and no-fault moral choices.

The list of absurd excuses can be seen in recent criminal defenses. For example, an Oregon man who tried to kill his ex-wife was acquitted on the grounds that he suffered from "depression-suicide syndrome," whose victims deliberately commit poorly planned crimes with the unconscious desire of being caught or killed. He didn't really want to shoot his wife; he wanted the police to shoot him. Or take the famous "Twinkie syndrome," a case that involved the attorneys of Dan White, who murdered San Francisco mayor George Moscone, who blamed the crime on Dan's emotional distress linked to his junk-food binges. Acquitted of murder, he was convicted on a lesser charge of manslaughter.

Pop psychology has conjured up so many new addictions that now no one can be held responsible for anything. We used to blame the devil. Then we blamed society. Today, we blame genetics. Now there is a new wave of biological determinism. As gene-mapping continues, we hear more and more about genetic determinants of behavior justifying our belief: "It's not my fault."

We have developed an elaborate excuse system. Three primary types of excuses are offered:

1. *I didn't do it.* This comes in the forms of denial, alibis, or blaming others. Adam and Eve used this one (Genesis 3:11-13), and so did Aaron when he made the golden calf (Exodus 32:24).

2. *It wasn't so bad.* This is minimization. "It was only a white lie," we tell ourselves. Here we justify and give good reasons for our misbehavior, such as King Saul did when he continued to disobey God (see 1 Samuel 15:13-15, 22).

3. *Yes, but. . . .* This is an admission of guilt followed by an excuse. It takes the form of "I couldn't help it," "I didn't mean to," or "It wasn't really me." "It was my mood, my personality or my temper," we say, as we separate ourselves from our actions. Jesus illustrated this excuse in His parable of the great banquet (Luke 14:18-20).

We have redefined *sin* in our day:

- Sin went to the psychiatrist and became "a disorder."
- Sin went to the doctor and became "a disease."
- Sin went to the sociologist and became "an environmental response."
- Sin went to the educator and became "a learning disorder."
- Sin went to the economist and became "financial discrimination."

God comes to each of us, as He did Adam and Eve in the Garden, and asks, "What have you done?" (See Genesis 3:13). He doesn't ask, "What have others done to you?" He doesn't ask, "What privileges have you been denied?" He doesn't ask, "Were you raised in a dysfunctional family?" He doesn't ask, "Has society treated you

unfairly?" He Asks, "What have *you* done?" This is not to discredit
the negative effect that our upbringing has on us, but what we have
done in response to it to take charge of our lives. We can't control
what has happened to us, but we can control our attitude and actions
in response to those things and decide that by the grace of God we
will rise above it. Only when we take charge of our lives and decide
to determine our destinies are we truly free to live the way God created us to live. I once read that we are God-created but self-molded.

Sometimes we make excuses rather than answer the call of God.
Like Moses, who told God at the burning bush, "I can't speak"
(Exodus 4:10). Or Gideon, who told the angel when God called him
to be a leader, "How can I save Israel? My clan is the weakest . . .
and I am the least in my family" (Judges 6:15). Or like Jeremiah,
who told God when called to be a prophet, "I am only a child" (1:6).
We all battle feelings of inadequacy, but if we take the challenge,
God will enable us by His grace to succeed.

It's time to stop making excuses and start setting an example!
There are three things I want you to know about taking charge of
your life.

I. We Are Free.
The first thing God told Adam when He put him in the Garden
was "you are free" (Genesis 2:16). God has endowed each of
us with the power of choice. The human will separates man
from the remainder of creation. We are more than biological
urges and instinctual responses—we are made in the image of
God, endowed with the power to think, to reason, to discriminate, to judge and to decide. All of that adds up to the power
of choice.

Having survived Hitler's death camps, psychiatrist Viktor
Frankl said, "The last of all human freedoms is the freedom to
choose one's attitude in any given set of circumstances."

Illustration

II. We Are Responsible.
Sometimes we try to assume responsibility for others, and we

end up frustrated because we can't live life for someone else. We are responsible to others, but we are not responsible for others. We have to consider how our choices affect other people. We need a deeper social consciousness that takes into consideration everyone who may be affected by our choices if we are to be mature. Immature people think of only themselves. Maturity considers others better than ourselves (Philippians 2:3). "Each of you should look not only to your own interests, but also to the interests of others" (v. 4).

Illustration

I heard about a pastor who gave up the ministry after 20 years to become a funeral director. When asked why he made the change he said, "Well, I spent about 12 years trying to straighten out John. He never did get straightened out. I spent 14 months trying to straighten out the marriage of the Smiths, and it never did get straightened out. I spent three years trying to straighten out Susan, and she never did get straightened out. *Now* when I straighten people out—they stay straight."

Illustration

In my first pastorate, I arrived late at the hospital emergency room in Athens, Georgia. Two young people had just been killed in a car crash caused by their own foolish choices. Disillusioned and angry, a group of teenagers asked me, "How could God allow this to happen?" I responded with understanding and yet clarity of truth: "God did not consume the substances or drive the car. This was the tragic result of human decisions."

III. We Are Accountable.

We are answerable to God in the Day of Judgment (see Matthew 12:37; Romans 14:10, 12; 2 Corinthians 3:10; 5:10; Hebrews 9:27). If we are in Christ, we do not need to fear judgment because Christ has pardoned our sins (1 John 4:17; Romans 8:1). But we do need to live our lives in a way that we can give an account that we sought to "walk worthy of the Lord and to please him in every way" (see Colossians 1:10) so that we can hear Him say, "Well, done, good and faithful servant" (Matthew 25:21, 23).

Leaven in the Lump

Text: 1 Corinthians 5:6-8

In many respects the quality of a person's life is determined by the influence of others, either positively or negatively. Let me ask you:

- Who are your heroes?
- Who are the mentors who have helped shape your life?
- What is your most significant childhood memory?
- What book has made the greatest impact in your life?
- What is the greatest compliment you've ever received?
- What is your favorite movie?
- Who are your closest friends?

All these questions share something in common—they all deal with significant experiences, events and persons who have influenced you. Each of us is, by and large, the product of influence. From the moment we are born we begin to be influenced. First, by our parents, and then our peers as we enter school. We are influenced by the marketplace, the church, the media, politics and the culture at large.

While we need positive influences, we need to guard against ungodly, negative influences. This was Paul's concern for the Corinthians when he wrote, "Don't you know that a little yeast works through the whole batch of dough?" (V. 6). He points out the same truth to the Galatians: "A little leaven leavens the whole lump" (5:9, *NKJV*).

Paul is drawing an allusion to the ancient Israelite celebration of the Passover and the Feast of Unleavened Bread, which lasted for the next seven days after the Passover (Exodus 12:8, 15; 13:7). Leaven, or yeast, is simply fermented bread used to lighten dough. Leaven also refers to any "pervasive influence that produces a significant change."

Throughout Scripture, leaven usually typifies sin (e.g., 12:15). Jesus also spoke of the leaven of religious self-righteousness, as did Paul, that robs us of spiritual joy and makes religion a burden (see Matthew 16:6, leaven of Pharisees and Sadducees; Mark 8:15, leaven of Pharisees and of Herod; Galatians 5:9, leaven of legalism).

What can we learn from the analogy of leaven and guarding our influences?

I.   Beware of the Subtlety of the Leaven.
   A.   *Sin possesses an innate subtlety.* Temptation often looks so innocent, so harmless, so much fun. Hebrews 11:25 reminds us that there is pleasure in sin for a short time. The Song of Solomon reminds us that "the little foxes . . . spoil the vines" (2:15, *NKJV*).
   B.   *Subtlety of social influences* (Proverbs 1:10; 1 Corinthians 15:33).

Illustration

When Harry Truman was thrust into the presidency by the death of Franklin Roosevelt, a friend took him aside and said: "From here on out, you're going to have lots of people around you. They'll try to put up a wall around you and cut you off from any ideas but theirs. They'll tell you what a great man you are, Harry. But you and I both know you ain't."

C. *Subtlety of intellectual influences.* We need to guard our minds (Proverbs 4:23; Philippians 4:8). We are constantly bombarded by secular ways of thinking contrary to God's Word that fill our minds with empty imaginations that we need to "take captive and make them obedient to Christ" (see 2 Corinthians 10:5).

D. *Subtlety of chemical influences.* America has more drug use, legal and illegal, than any other country. It's easy to develop a dependency without realizing it, and then a person is in bondage to a substance.

II. Understand the Far-Reaching Effects of the Leaven.

A. *Leaven has a permeating effect.* It works through the whole batch of dough. Sin, legalism, or whatever negative form of leaven we want to discuss is never localized. It's like cancer; it spreads, it permeates, and brings the total life under its influence if left unchecked. Gossip spreads. Lack of faith spreads. The 10 spies who gave a bad report when spying out the land of Canaan caused their unbelief to spread through nearly the whole camp of Israel. Their hearts melted with fear, and they refused to possess the land and ended up in the wilderness for 40 years. The leaven of unbelief from 10 men affected nearly 2 million people. Do the math and decide whether or not it is important for us to be positive, faith-filled people. I think you will agree with me that we cannot afford to think, speak and act in unbelief regarding the promises of God.

B. *Generational curses* (Exodus 20:5). The sins of fathers affect up to the third and fourth generations. This does not mean that God punishes us for the sins of our fathers but that their sins continue to impact us because of the consequences of sin. The sin of slavery is still impacting our nation with the racial and ethnic discrimination. Generational curses in the Bible (which, by the way, is only mentioned here in the Ten Commandments, Exodus 20:5) do not speak of a curse in

voodoo or witchcraft, but rather the transference of sins from
generation to generation through modeling. Individuals of
every generation can decide to end the curse if they assume
responsibility and decide by grace they are not going to carry
on the sins of previous generations.

C. *The far-reaching effects of the Kingdom.* Jesus said the
kingdom of God is like leaven, which works through the
dough. We can inject the leaven of faith, hope and love
into our families, our world, our businesses and see the
powerful impact of the Kingdom (Matthew 13:33).

III. Remove the Old Leaven Swiftly and Thoroughly.

When it comes to leaven as sin or something negative, we
need to learn three lessons:

A. *Examination.* The day before the Passover, the Jews lit a
candle and thoroughly searched their homes for every
crumb of leaven. We get the picture of God making His
search of His people in Zephaniah 1:12: "At that time I
will search Jerusalem with lamps and punish those who
are complacent . . . who think, 'The Lord will do nothing,
either good or bad.' " We need the Holy Spirit to make the
search in our hearts for any leaven (Psalm 139:23, 24).

B. *Elimination.* "Get rid of the old yeast," Paul tells us clearly (1 Corinthians 5:7). What is in your life that you need
to get rid of? Paul gives us a list of things we need to get
rid of in Ephesians 4:31.

C. *Encouragement.* Paul says the reason we need to get rid
of the leaven is so "that you may be a new batch without
yeast—as you really are" (1 Corinthians 5:7). The leaven
of sin and immaturity hinders us from living up to our
potential.

The Light of the World

G.K. Chesterton once said, "There is only one thing certain about man—that man is not what he was meant to be." The Bible says, "All have sinned and fall short of the glory of God" (Romans 3:23). Sin basically means "to miss the mark; to deviate from God's plan; to depart from God's will."

The result of sin is a darkened world. We stagger in spiritual darkness without a sense of direction, lost in our way and frightened by our own spiritual condition. The Bible uses the analogy of darkness to describe the effects of sin and alienation from God (Proverbs 4:18, 19; John 3:19; 2 Corinthians 4:4; Ephesians 4:18; 1 John 2:11).

Hell itself is described as a place of outer darkness (Matthew 25:30). Most children are afraid of the dark. Most crimes are committed in the dark. Darkness itself can be a frightening experience. Myles Donnely, who escaped from the 78th floor of the South Tower in the 9/11 tragedy, said, "It sounds an awful thing for a grown man to say, but I think I am afraid of the dark again."

In the midst of a world of darkness shines the light of Christ. The coming of Jesus into the world and into our lives is the entrance of light. *Light* is a form of radiant energy consisting of electromagnetic waves of various lengths. The eye responds to these different wavelengths, converting them to colors. The human can distinguish 8 million colors. Light travels at the speed of 186,000 mps, which is 670,615,600 mph. It takes the light of the sun, which is 92,800,000 miles away, eight minutes to reach Earth.

As incredible as it may seem, it takes the light of the closest star to Earth, Proxima Centauri, 4.25 years to reach Earth. We have learned to harness the light rays of radio waves, X-rays, ultraviolet and infrared waves to enrich our lives. Light controls evil by providing protection—crime lights, streetlights. Light directs a lost traveler, such as a lighthouse or, as we say, the light at the end of a tunnel. But the most important quality of light is its life-giving power. All green plants derive their growth from light and, in turn, provide food and oxygen for animals and mankind.

The first act of Creation was the emergence of light (Genesis 1:1-4). Once light came, life followed. Light refers to the spiritual life. Jesus proclaimed, "I am the light of the world" (John 8:12; 9:5). What does that announcement mean to us?

I.   The Setting

A.   He made this announcement at the Feast of Tabernacles. This annual festival, which lasted for seven days every fall, commemorated the exodus of Israel from Egypt and the wilderness experience.

B.   Jesus made this statement while in the Temple area known as the Treasury, where people brought their gifts. The Treasury was part of a larger court known as the Court of Women. At the close of the first day of the festival, a dramatic ceremony took place in this court. Four great candelabra were prepared for lighting. When evening came the people flocked to the court for the candle-lighting ceremony. At dark, as four youths of priestly lineage were given the signal to light the candelabra, suddenly the darkness was dispelled.

C. It is said that every street and court and square in Jerusalem
was illuminated by the light. On one particular night, as the
light illuminated the city, Jesus lifted His voice: "I am the
light of the world!"

II. The Significance

What did the candelabra mean to the people?

A. The light reminded them of the pillar of fire that guided
and protected them in the desert.

B. The light represented the Shekinah glory of God that appeared as a luminous, glowing, radiant mist in the Tabernacle, and
later at the dedication of Solomon's temple.

C. The light spoke of the coming of Messiah, of whom Isaiah
said, "The people walking in darkness have seen a great light;
on those living in the land of the shadow of death a light has
dawned" (9:2). Jesus was declaring Himself as Messiah
when He said "I am the light." He was the One who would
guide and protect His people. He is the glory of God revealed
among us, who takes up His residence in our hearts and fills
us with God's glory. And He will deliver us from the darkness of sin, guilt and fear.

III. The Spirituality

What does this mean to us spiritually?

A. *A light for the world.* The word *world*, which is *kosmos* in
Greek, speaks of both the earth (Psalm 24:1) and humanity in rebellion to God (1 John 2:15-17). Most important,
it means the world in need of salvation. "God so loved the
world" (John 3:16).

B. *A light to be followed.* The call of Christ is "Follow me"
(Matthew 4:19). *To follow* means to go the same direction,
to be a close companion, to surrender our will to Him. We
are to follow the Light of the World if we are to live with
direction and purpose. If you were lost in the woods at
night and had a flashlight, you would simply walk in the

steps of path the light would make in front of you. The beam of light would form a path of light for you to follow in the darkness. We don't need to fear the darkness of this world or get lost in it. All we need to do is follow Christ, the Light of life.

C. *A light to be experienced.* Jesus is "the light of life" (John 8:12). When Paul met Christ on the road to Damascus, he was blinded by the brilliant light in his vision of Christ. Light had shone into his life, and the darkness was gone.

Illustration

At the end of World War II, King George VI delivered an address to the British Commonwealth on Christmas Eve in a palace in London. He challenged Britain's leaders to faith: "I said to the man at the Gate of the Year, 'Give me a light that I may walk safely into the unknown.' He said to me, 'Go out into the darkness, and put your hand in the hand of God, and it shall be to you better than the light, and safer than the known.'" At the time he spoke these words, his listeners knew he was dying of cancer. There was an anchor to his own soul in the time of need (Ravi Zacharias, *Can Man Live Without God?*, p. 53).

Closing: He is the Light of the World!

Born in a Manger ... Raised on a Cross

Christmas Sermon

Text: John 3:16

The most celebrated holiday of the year is Christmas. We travel back to Bethlehem in our minds to experience the scene of the Christ in the manger. We try to imagine what that holy night must have really been like for those who experienced it (Luke 2:8-14).

When we go to Israel, we always visit the traditional site in Bethlehem where the birth of Jesus is believed to have taken place in the ruins of an ancient stable formed out of rock. We also visit the church where Jerome translated the Bible into Latin, which is called the Latin Vulgate (c. A.D. 400).

There is something comforting about the Christ in the manger. But can we really grasp the meaning of the manger apart from the Cross? Calvary, after all, is the fulfillment of the manger. He was born in a manger but raised on a cross. This is what He meant when He said to Nicodemus, the Pharisee, who came to see Him alone one night: "As Moses lifted up the serpent in the wilderness, even so must the Son of Man be lifted up" (John 3:14).

Reinhold Neibuhr, in *The Kingdom of God in America,* said,
"We want a God without wrath who took man without sin into a
kingdom without justice through the ministrations of a Christ without a cross." But regardless of how hard we try, we can't escape the
words of John 3:16: "For God so loved the world that He gave His
only begotten Son" (*NKJV*). And He gave Him on a cross. He was
born in a manger to be raised on a cross.

I. God So Loved.

  A. Today God is on trial. Is God as good as Jesus? This was
       important to Nicodemus who was a Pharisee. There were
       about 6,000 Pharisees in Christ's day. They held to rab-
       binic tradition—the party of the synagogue that practiced
       strict legalism. They believed in the supernatural (angels,
       demons), in the Resurrection, and expected the apocalyp-
       tic coming of the kingdom of God. While they had some
       good qualities, they basically saw God as Lawgiver and
       not as Love.

  B. What is God like? Religions have always struggled with
       this issue:

      1. To the Egyptian, God is immortality.
      2. To the Hebrew, He is righteous law.
      3. To the Hindu, He is truth and bliss.
      4. To the Buddhist, God is the force of life in the universe.
      5. To the ancient Greek, He is wisdom.
      6. To the Muslim, God is authority.
      7. To the humanist, God is the power of human potential.
      8. To the scientist, He is natural law.

  C. In Christianity, God is Love (1 John 4:16)! But not just
       any kind of love, and not love as an abstract idea, but a
       concrete action: "This is how God showed his love among
       us: He sent his one and only Son into the world that we
       might live through him. This is love: not that we loved
       God, but that God loved us and sent his Son as an atoning
       sacrifice for our sins" (vv. 9, 10). Here is one of the great-
       est statements in the Bible: "God demonstrates his own

love for us in this: While we were still sinners, Christ died
for us" (Romans 5:8).

II. God So Loved the World.

A. If the first statement wasn't enough, the follow-up defi-
nitely caught Nicodemus off guard—God so loved *the
world*. The world? Surely he expected Jesus to say God
loved the righteous, or the covenant people, or the nation
of Israel. But the world? The world included everyone—
pagans, idolaters, and even Rome, the enemy of Israel.
For centuries, Israel had been subject to one Gentile
power after another, always fighting for their freedom and
trying to preserve their religious and cultural distinctive-
ness. Did God love the enemies of Israel? Did God love
King Herod? Caesar?

B. Jesus was including Nicodemus in the world. The
Pharisees saw themselves as spiritually superior. But Jesus
put the good and bad in the category of needing redemption. John the Baptist did the same thing when he called for
the Jews to be baptized and to repent. We all have a common problem, sin, and a common solution, Jesus Christ.
Augustine said, "God loves each of us as though there
were only one of us to love." We stand equal at the foot of
the Cross. This is why no one should judge another. We are
all sinners in need of saving grace.

III. God So Loved the World That He Gave His Only Son.

How are we to measure the love of God? Love came in the
incarnation of Jesus Christ. Love was made flesh and dwelt
among us.

A. *Jesus is the expression of the love of God.* Without Jesus,
love becomes sentimental. But He fleshes it out so that we
can see it, touch it and feel it. In 1 John the word *love* is
used 43 times. The word *this* is used 29 times as a way of
defining the love of God specifically in Christ.

B. *Jesus is the essence of God.* Here we see the divinity of
Jesus: the Son of God, who is coexistent, eternal and equal

with the Father. "I and my Father are one," He said (John 10:30, KJV).

C. *Jesus is God's gift to us.* The word *grace* means "to give freely." How did God give Him? On a cross. E.S. Jones writes of a Hindu who commented on the difference between Hinduism and Christianity: "The difference between Hinduism and Christianity is this: We have to climb the ladder of austerity to get to Brahma. He doesn't lift his finger to help us. In Christianity, God comes to the bottom rung at cost, the cost of a cross, to help us to the topmost rung. The difference is decisive" (E.S. Jones, *Christian Maturity*, p. 37). All we need to do to be saved from our sins and have eternal life is to receive the gift of Christ.

IV. Whoever Believes in Him

A. *Whoever.* This may be the most important verse in the Bible—*whoever*. I accidentally ended up in downtown Atlanta as a college student at the site of the first gay rights rally in the '70s. I was going to a convention at the World Congress Center and just happened to get there at the same time the rally was in the same area. They were protesting the Christian gathering being held at the World Congress Center. I noticed a sign being held high above the crowd by a young man that read: "Jesus died for somebody's sins, but it wasn't for mine." What a tragedy. He had missed the good news of Christ somewhere along the line. But the truth is, Jesus did die for his sins and for ours as well. The invitation is to whoever (see John 6:37; Revelation 22:17).

B. *Believes.* This involves personal faith based on personal revelation. Like the centurion at the cross, Jesus died for your sins, not just the world's sin. This is the result of faith:
    1. What will not happen—you will not perish.
    2. What will happen—you will have everlasting life!

Does God Want Me to Be Happy?

Text: Psalm 1

Blaise Pascal wrote, "All men seek happiness. This is without exception. Whatever different means they employ, they all tend to this end. This is the motive of every action of every man, even of those who hang themselves." Everybody wants to be happy. Whether you are 7, 17 or 70, you want to be happy. We may call it by different names—success, joy, fulfillment, peace of mind, significance. But we all want it. Americans especially have a pre-occupation with happiness. Even the Declaration of Independence states that we have been endowed "with certain unalienable rights, that among these are life, liberty and the pursuit of happiness." Many never do find happiness. As Thoreau said, "The mass of men lead lives of quiet desperation."

To be happy means "to be content; to be satisfied; to be pleased with one's state in life." What does it take to be happy? According to psychological research, Americans identify four key ingredients to happiness: to be loved and accepted; to be comfortable; to have security; and to make a difference. When we ask the question, we get a variety of responses because different factors make different people happy. For some, happiness is making good money, finding a mate, having children, raising a family, a career change, financial security, or good health.

When the Scripture talks about happiness, it uses the word *blessed.* The Scripture is clear that the key to the secret of happiness is from the blessing of God. The word *blessed* has several aspects of meaning:

* The favor of the Lord; literally, "to speak well of"
* To convey gifts upon
* The blessing opposes and nullifies the curse of the law and sin. Outside of blessing, man lives under the curse of sin (Ecclesiastes 1:2).
* The fullness and abundance of life
* The enjoyment of life. David expresses this truth in the first psalm, which sets the tone for the entire psalter. He begins with the statement, "Blessed is the man." Blessedness is a gift from God. It is not contingent on our life situation. No level of adversity or trouble can take away God's blessings.

Psalm 1 is a wisdom psalm that calls us to godly living. Godliness is the key to happiness. Like Proverbs and Ecclesiastes, the Psalms are Hebrew wisdom literature. Wisdom gives us perspective in a world of sin and suffering. Life is tough! But God knows and cares. Psalm 1 introduces the Psalms and states unequivocally that God blesses those who are faithful to Him.

I.   Eliminate the Negatives (v. 1).

    A.   *The way of the ungodly.* The terms *ungodly, sinners* and *scornful (NKJV)* convey the totality of evil. To be happy we must disassociate with the world. The three action verbs *walk, stand* and *sit* are to be understood in their contrast to a life of loving obedience (Deuteronomy 6:7).

        1.   *Beliefs.* Do not walk in the counsel of the ungodly: scheme, advice, plans, patterns of the wicked (*rasha*); literally means "to be out of joint," or out of step with God.

2. *Behavior.* Do not stand in the way of sinners: *chatta* means "to miss the mark; a mistaking of the way; habitual sinning."

3. *Belonging.* Do not sit in the seat of mockers: *lesim*, "a cynical and arrogant contempt for God; scornful." This is the self-sufficient man who boasts of his complete independence from God. The mocker is called a fool in the Wisdom Literature (Proverbs 14:9). He does not respond to instruction, he stirs up strife by his insults and delights in his mockery of God.

B. *The way of the righteous.* They walk, stand and sit in ways that are devoted to the Lord (Deuteronomy 6:7). The godly keep a distance between themselves and the world system lest they come under its influence (1 John 2:15-17). Someone asked D.L. Moody if they would have to give up the world if they became a Christian. He replied, "No. The world will give you up." We live by a higher standard than the world.

A good friend of mine was a helicopter pilot in Vietnam. He trained pilots in instrument flying. He told me about a time he flew in a terrible storm. He began to experience a sense of disorientation and felt like the plane was falling. He had zero visibility. He just kept his eyes on the instruments and flew by the instrument readings and ignored his feelings. The only thing you have to operate on is your instruments. You keep your focus on your instrument readings and fly by those readings regardless of what you feel. Even so, we "fly" by the instrument of the law of the Lord in spite of feelings, desires and temptations, doubts and uncertainties, and the voice of the world.

Illustration

II. Accentuate the Positive (vv. 2-5).

A. *The Law.* The Law (Torah) can be used of the Pentateuch, the Old Testament as a whole, or the entire Bible. It primarily speaks of instruction that comes from God rooted in the Scripture. As Christians we are to seek to fulfill the will of God as revealed in Jesus, who is the fulfillment of the Law (Matthew 5:17).

B. *The Lifestyle*

1. *Delight (hepso).* "His delight is in the law of the Lord" (Psalm 1:2). He does not use the word *duty* or even *discipline* but, rather, *delight*. The word *delight* describes all that makes a man happy. The law is the godly man's desire (112:1; Isaiah 58:13, 14). Job said, "I have esteemed the words of his mouth more than my necessary food" (23:12, KJV). Jeremiah said, "Your words were found, and I ate them, and Your word was to me the joy and rejoicing of my heart" (15:16, *NKJV*). David said, "Oh, how I love your law! I meditate on it all day long" (Psalm 119:97). Jesus said His words are to remain in us (John 15:7). Paul said the word of Christ should dwell in us (Colossians 3:16).

2. *Meditate (hagah).* This means to saturate the mind and the spirit with the Word of God. Have you ever watched a cow chew its cud? That's meditation! The word literally means "to mutter or to murmur" and alludes to the sound of animals or to a moaning noise (see Isaiah 16:7). The ancient Jews memorized the Scripture with low murmuring sounds to intensify concentration. At the Wailing Wall in Jerusalem, you can see the rabbis reading the Law and muttering sounds as they are memorizing the passages. In ancient times, people did not have copies of the Scripture, so they committed it to memory. They spent time pondering the works of the Lord and reflecting on His greatness. It is interesting to note that such meditation does not refer to setting aside special time for the study of the Scriptures but, rather, the reflection of the Word in the course of daily activities (Joshua 1:8; Deuteronomy 6:7).

3. *Obey.* The whole purpose of delighting and meditating in the law of God is to do His will so that whatever

comes our way, we can respond in a way that glorifies God (James 1:22-25).

C. *The portrait of happiness is seen in the Tree of Life.*

    1. The first image of the godly is that they will be like the Tree of Life in Eden (Genesis 2:9; Revelation 2:7). In Psalm 1:3 the phrase "planted by streams of water" represents the continual supply of the Holy Spirit. The phrase "yields its fruit" means we are blessed and prospered by God. The phrase "leaf does not wither" means we are protected from curse and drought.

    2. This does not mean we are to pursue success as an end in itself. We are to seek God himself and His will. Happiness is a by-product of obedience. Neither does this mean that godliness ensures a trouble-free life. It means that we can expect the blessings of God in the midst of whatever comes our way.

D. *"Not so the wicked!"*

    1. How stark these words stand in contrast to the portrait of blessing on the people of God." They are like chaff that the wind blows away" (v. 4). The imagery of chaff is used frequently in Scripture (35:5; Isaiah 17:13; Hosea 13:3; Zephaniah 2:2; Matthew 3:12).

    2. Malachi sees the end of the wicked on the Day of the Lord as stubble and a tree consumed by fire (4:1). The phrase "the wind blows away" means no one will remember the wicked in a positive. They make no lasting contribution. What a contrast to the godly whose leaf never withers.

    3. Furthermore, the wicked are alienated from the eternal blessings of God. They have no future: They cannot stand in the Judgment or sit in the assembly of the righteous (i.e., the people of God). *Judgment* refers to the whole judicial process by which God will establish His rule on earth.

III. Remember the Bottom Line (v. 6).

A. "The Lord watches over the way of the righteous, but the way of the wicked will perish." The concept of *way* means one's manner of life. God knows! God sees all; He knows how we live. No one can escape the all-seeing eye of God.

B. Bette Midler sings, "God is watching us from a distance." But the truth is, "His eye is on the sparrow, and I know He watches me." "The Lord watches over the way of the righteous" means that He loves and cares for us and that He will reward us.

C. The concept is also that of knowing. The Lord knows the way that we take, which means He is intimately connected with us the way Adam and Eve knew each other. The deliverance of Israel from Egypt began with the knowledge of God about their suffering. God's knowledge is a deep commitment to loving and caring for His own (Romans 8:35-39).

Faithful Fathers
Father's Day Sermon

Text: Psalm 15

A s we look at the landscape of the American family today, we are prone to ask, "Where have all the fathers gone?" It seems that fathers have done a disappearing act from their families. Some fathers have disappeared physically—their presence is absent from the lives of their children through separation, divorce or abandonment. Some have disappeared emotionally—so caught up in their personal pursuits that they have little time for their children to provide the support and nurture needed. Most tragically, many have disappeared spiritually—abdicated their place as the priest of the home, the church and the community.

Can there be any higher calling than to be a father? After all, the highest revelation of God is the fatherhood of God. When a man becomes a father, he steps into the calling of reflecting the fatherhood of God to his children. You aren't going to learn about fatherhood from the secular trends of the day; you have to look to the heavenly Father for your cues.

Bill Keane, creator of the *Family Circus* cartoon strip, tells of a time when he was penciling one of his cartoons and his son, Jeffy, said, "Daddy, how do you know what to draw?" He replied, "God tells me." Jeffy said, "Then why do you keep on erasing parts of it?"

What areas of life do fathers need to watch if they are going to be men of God in such secular times and make a difference in the lives of their children?

I.   Character (v. 2a)

    A. *Character* means the moral force or integrity of one's life. Today we hear a lot about the fact that character doesn't count. But it counts with God. Character is more important than power, prestige, position, possessions and pleasure.

    B. The most important pursuit of any man's life is the pursuit of holy character (Galatians 5:22, 23). The spiritual man of Psalm 15 is contrasted with the secular man of Psalm 14: "The fool says in his heart, 'There is no God' " (v. 1).

Oscar Wilde came to the United States for a visit in 1882. When asked by customs if he had anything to declare, he replied, "Only my genius." Fifteen years later, alone and broke and in prison, he reflected on his life of waste and excess. He wrote: "I have been a spendthrift of my genius. . . . I forgot that every little action of the common day makes or unmakes character."

A Careful Man (anonymous)

    A careful man I want to be; a little fellow follows me.
    I do not care to go astray, for fear he'll go the selfsame way.
    I cannot once escape his eyes; whatever he sees me do, he tries.
    Like me he says he's going to be, this little lad who follows me.
    He thinks that I am good and fine; believes in every word of mine.
    The base in me he must not see, this little lad who follows me.
    I must remember as I go, through summer's sun and winter's snow,
    I'm building for the years to be, this little fellow who follows me.

II. Communication (v. 2b)

Communication is a dynamic process of interaction involving talking, listening and understanding. Communication is simply conversation with a purpose. We need to eliminate negative communication and practice positive communication (see Ephesians 4:29). The goal of all communication should be to communicate love to our children.

Paul Budd, in *God's Vitamin "C."* tells of a lesson he learned from a young poet:

> As I reviewed my son's papers from school one night last week, I came across one paper with a failing grade. I almost came up out of my chair. I started to yell his name when I suddenly realized he was in bed asleep. It didn't matter that this was only his second year of school. At that moment I saw his academic career in ruins. I was angry. But I put the paper aside and turned to the next one. It had some pencil scribbles, and at the top of the page was written, "My Dad." It was a poem about me.
>
> His poem included the time I had to leave work to take him to the doctor because he had broken his finger. I had forgotten about that. He talked about how I wrestled with him in the evenings. And he talked about a few other things he likes that I do.
>
> That paper with the failing grade was suddenly not nearly as important as it had been just a few minutes earlier. I don't know if he planted the poem next to the failing grade in order to soften the blow, but it worked. Instead of a severe lecture, I talked to him about the poem as well as the failed assignment.
>
> It began to make sense to me that I could include praise along with constructive criticism. I got the idea from a poem I read (*Bits and Pieces,* June 1998, p. 9).

Illustration

III. Companionships (v. 3)

Our relationships shape our lives. Our relationships make us or break us. We are to avoid the counsel of the ungodly (1:1), surround ourselves with wise counselors (Proverbs 13:20), and guard the company we keep (1 Corinthians 15:33).

IV. Commitments (v. 4)

A. Keeping your commitments is the key to pleasing God and experiencing true success (Ecclesiastes 5:1-7).

B. Men of God need to be marked as men of their word. Every time I perform a wedding, I am reminded of the level of commitment it takes to be married: "for better or worse, for richer or poorer, in sickness and in health . . . till death us do part."

C. *Commitment,* I once read, means doing what you said you would do long after the feeling you had when you said it is gone.

V. Commerce (v. 5)

A. It has been said that you write your autobiography in your checkbook. Jesus tells us that our money reveals our hearts (Matthew 6:19-21).

B. Let us listen again to the counsel of the Word about the love of money (1 Timothy 6:6-10). Most importantly, Solomon tells us, "Honor the Lord with your wealth" (Proverbs 3:9, 10).

Illustration

John Wesley, while preaching on money, said, "Make all the money you can." A man said a hearty "Amen!" Wesley continued, "Save all the money you can." Again the man said, "Amen!" Wesley said, "Give all the money you can." The man turned to the person next to him and said, "Why did he have to go ruin a good sermon?"

After a 23-year career with the IRS, Anne Sheiber retired from her job in 1944. During her years of service, she had never earned more than $4,000 a year and never received a promotion, despite having a law degree and leading her office in turning up underpayments and underreporting. When she retired, she took her savings of $5,000 and invested it in the stock market. Some 50 years later, in January 1995, Anne died at age 101. By that time her $5,000 investment had grown to $22 million in stocks. She had made all her investment decisions scouring *The Wall Street Journal* every day, and her portfolio included such companies as Coca-Cola and Paramount. She willed all of her stockholdings to Yeshiva University in New York—a university that had never even heard of her. Here was a lady who invested for the future (from Pat Williams, *The Magic of Teamwork,* cited in *Bits and Pieces,* Jan. 18, 1998, p. 24).

C. Here's the promise to the man of God: "He who does these things will never be shaken." The psalmist describes what it means to live as men of God in Psalm 15. He describes the man who cannot be shaken. That's what we need today at home—unshakable men. We need men whose faith cannot be shaken in the face of life's disappointments; whose hope cannot be shaken in times of despair; whose love cannot be shaken in times of injustice; whose convictions cannot be shaken in times of compromise; whose joy cannot be shaken in times of depression; whose peace cannot be shaken in times of fear; whose confidence cannot be shaken in times of uncertainty; and whose commitments cannot be shaken in times of unfaithfulness.

Closing: Michele Gold, in *Gratitude: A Way of Life,* told about a father who gave his young daughter a simple locket and told her that it contained a very valuable diamond sealed inside the locket, so if at any time she was ever in need, she could crack open the locket, sell the diamond, and make it through difficult times.

The daughter grew up and later struggled through tough financial times; but just the thought of the diamond resting safely around her neck gave her enough courage to pull through. Many years later she became successful and no longer struggled to survive. Her curiosity finally got the best of her, and she wanted to know how much the diamond was actually worth.

She took the diamond to a jeweler to have it appraised. She watched anxiously as he eyed the plain, tarnished lock with a bit of skepticism. He raised his mallet and, with one swift blow, smashed the little locket into many pieces. There was the small, smooth clear stone. The jeweler held it up to the light and said, "Why this isn't a diamond, my lady, it's a worthless piece of ordinary glass!" Stunned by his words, the woman laughed, then cried, and then laughed again.

"No sir," she said, "it's not worthless," as she wiped the tears from her eyes. "It's the most beautiful and valuable diamond in the world." Her father had given her a priceless gem . . . the gift of hope and the belief that you can make it regardless of the difficulties you face (*Bits and Pieces,* Jan. 18, 1998, pp. 22-23).

Blessed Is the Nation
July Fourth Sermon

Text: Psalm 33

A braham Lincoln once referred to America as the "last, best hope of the earth." Why would he make such a statement? Perhaps it was because America was forged out of the furnace of faith in God. Whether we like it or not, America's roots are spiritual. The Liberty Bell has the words from Leviticus inscribed on it: "Proclaim liberty throughout all the land unto all the inhabitants thereof" (25:10, KJV).

When Christopher Columbus set sail for the Indies, he said that God was guiding his steps. He felt that he had been inspired by the Holy Spirit so that the light of Christ might shine to those without Him.

When the Pilgrims came to America aboard the Mayflower, they sought to establish a land for the glory of God with full freedom of worship. The Mayflower Compact, developed by the Pilgrims on the Mayflower who came to the Plymouth Rock Colony in the winter of 1620, clearly says that the purpose for establishing the colony was "for the glory of God and the advancement of the Christian faith, and honor of our King and country."

On July 4, 1776, the Declaration of Independence, authored by Thomas Jefferson, was adopted by the Second Continental Congress consisting of 56 delegates. Above all, it underscores our foundation of faith: "We hold these truths to be self-evident, that all men are created equal, that they are endowed by their Creator with certain unalienable Rights, that among these are Life, Liberty and the pursuit of Happiness. . . . And for the support of this Declaration, with a firm reliance on the protection of Divine Providence, we mutually pledge to each other our Lives, our Fortunes and our sacred Honor."

Daniel Webster said, "Whatever makes men good Christians makes them good citizens." And Jacques Auguste de Thou remarked, "After what I owe to God, nothing should be more dear or more sacred to me than the love and respect I owe my country."

The question today is, "Will America continue to be a nation of faith, or will we go the way of empires before us?" As far as the church is concerned, we ask ourselves, "What role are we to play in the spiritual revitalization of America?" Suddenly Psalm 33 takes on special significance for our times. The psalmist lays down a timeless truth for every nation: "Blessed is the nation whose God is the Lord" (v. 12).

God is concerned about nations: Genesis 12:3; Psalm 9:17; 46:10; Proverbs 14:34; 29:2; Isaiah 2:2 ("all nations will stream to [the Lord's Temple]"); 56:7 ("a house of prayer for all nations"); Haggai 2:7 ("the desired of all nations will come"); Matthew 24:14; 28:19; Revelation 21:24.

What do we need to do for America?

I.   Celebrate God's Goodness to the Nation (vv. 1-5).

A.   *Our National Day of Thanksgiving.* The first Thanksgiving Day was held in Newfoundland in 1578 by an English minister named Wolfall. Another was celebrated in 1607; then again at Plymouth Rock Colony in 1621 with the Pilgrims and at least 90 Indians who feasted together for three days. On November 26, 1789, George Washington proclaimed the first national day by stating, "Whereas it is the duty of all nations to acknowledge the providence of Almighty God, to obey His will, to be grateful for His benefits and humbly implore His protection and favor." Sarah J. Hale sent a copy of Washington's proclamation to Abraham Lincoln, insisting that he follow suit, which he did. He proclaimed July 15, 1863, a national day of thanksgiving, three days after the Battle of Gettysburg. The Congress ratified the decision in 1941 to declare the last Thursday of November. Every president since that time has declared a day of thanksgiving.

B. *The goodness of God.* "Good and upright is the Lord; therefore he instructs sinners in his ways" (Psalm 25:8). "The Lord is good to all; he has compassion on all he has made" (145:9). Nahum 1:7 says, "The Lord is good, a refuge in times of trouble. He cares for those who trust in him." James 1:17 says, "Every good and perfect gift is from above."

II. Affirm God's Sovereignty Over the Nation (vv. 12-15).

A. Here are three significant statements in this passage:

1. God chose us as His inheritance (v. 12).

2. God looks down on us from heaven and watches over us from His "dwelling place" (v. 14), or "throne" (see Revelation 4:1-3).

3. He forms the hearts and considers everything we do (Psalm 33:15).

B. The colonists boldly declared as they rebelled against the tyranny of England, "No king but King Jesus!" It is interesting to note that in the language of the Constitution the makers lack any use of the words *sovereign* or *sovereignty.* They realized that only God was absolutely sovereign. All the framers of the Constitution, except one, were Christians: 19 were Episcopalians; eight were Congregationalists; seven were Presbyterians; two were Roman Catholics; two were Quakers; one was a Methodist; one was a Dutch Reformed. The deist believed that God existed, but that He pretty much left us to our own devices. Note that not one was an atheist.

    C. The First Amendment was specifically designed to prohibit the intrusion of the state into the affairs of the church, as was the case with the Church of England when the Pilgrims left.

Illustration

When Abraham Lincoln was assassinated, most of this country went into mourning. There was confusion, despair and hopelessness. In New York City, a crowd gathered. They expressed the loss of the president and their concern about the future. Suddenly, a man climbed up the stairs of a building where he could look over the crowd and shouted with a loud voice, "The Lord reigns over Washington!" The people grew silent as the meaning of his words reassured them. Slowly they began to disperse and go about their business.

III. Trust in God's Providence Over the Nation (vv. 16-22).

    A. *The providence of God.* Here we learn four things about God:
        1. The Lord looks down from heaven (v. 13).
        2. He considers everything we do (v. 15).
        3. "The eyes of the Lord are on those who fear him" (v. 18).
        4. He delivers us from death and keeps us alive in famine (v. 19).

    B. *The powerlessness of man.* "No king is saved by the size of his army; no warrior escapes by his great strength. A horse is a vain hope for deliverance; despite all its great strength it cannot save" (vv. 16, 17).

    C. Here is our response to God's providential care:
        1. We wait for the Lord (v. 20).
        2. We trust in His holy name (v. 21).
        3. We put our hope in Him (v. 22).

Illustration

The voyage of Christopher Columbus illustrates the principle of perseverance. I'm sure every crew member who sailed with Columbus began the voyage to the New World with unswerving confidence. However, as days turned to weeks, and weeks to months, their confidence turned to fear, and fear to mutiny. But Columbus sailed on. He simply would not be denied. And his dream became reality. And so can yours.

The Lord Needs It!
Palm Sunday Sermon

Text: Mark 11:1-11

What an incredible sight it was that day. The Passover was at hand. Hundreds of thousands of Jewish pilgrims had returned from all over the world to celebrate the festival in Jerusalem. Passover marked the celebration of their deliverance from bondage in Egypt. But there was something unique about this Passover. Many believed that another day of deliverance was at hand—the deliverance from Roman oppression. Since 63 B.C., Rome had controlled Israel. The people were weary with the oppression of Rome.

The people longed for a deliverer. They longed for the Old Testament promise of a Messiah to be fulfilled. Now, that day had come. Jesus of Nazareth had filled Israel with the Word of God and the miracles of God. His message was clear and filled with hope: "Repent, for the kingdom of heaven is near" (Matthew 4:17). The message was confirmed by His miracles.

The Passover began in a most unusual way. Jesus entered Jerusalem riding on a donkey, just as Zechariah said the Messiah would (9:9). The donkey is a symbol of peace for a king. He came in peace and for peace. The donkey was an honorable animal in the ancient world. Jesus fulfilled Zechariah's prophecy. His actions spoke volumes of Zechariah's declaration of the Messiah. The people laid their garments on the ground before Him, just as had been done for Jehu when he was anointed king of Israel (2 Kings 9:13).

The Triumphal Entry was a paradox. On one hand, it was a time of praise and anticipation. On the other hand, it was a time of disappointment when Jesus failed to be the Messiah they wanted— one who would take on the Roman government. Within a week some in that same crowd would shout, "Crucify Him!"

The people lined the street by the thousands, waving palm branches in praise and celebration, declaring, "Hosanna!" The word is a cry for help and deliverance, meaning "Save now!" "Blessed is he who comes in the name of the Lord!" they proclaimed as they hailed Him their Messiah (Mark 11:9). "He who comes" is a phrase they used for the Messiah. The shouts of "Hosanna" are recorded in Psalm 118:26. This psalm is used in the Passover, the Feast of Tabernacles and other great celebrations. It is a psalm of conquest and victory and shows their limited understanding of the Messiah.

Praise is more than shouts of joy or songs of celebration. *Praise is the giving of ourselves to Him* in unreserved love and commitment to His purpose in our lives. Real praise goes beyond declaration to dedication. Among the celebration that day was a man who understood such praise. He was the man who gave his donkey for Jesus to ride. Jesus sent two disciples into town with instructions that they would see a donkey tied up at a certain home. They were to take it and bring it to Him. If anyone asked them what they were doing, they were to reply, "The Lord needs it" (v. 3). Jesus had arranged for this with the owner of the donkey in advance. The phrase "The Lord needs it" was the question. He calls us to surrender ourselves to Him for His service and ministry (Joshua 24:15; Luke 9:23; Romans 12:1; Philippians 1:21).

You may be saying to yourself, "I have so little to offer Him." God has been taking our little and doing a lot with it since the beginning of time. God is able to do "exceedingly, abundantly above all that we ask or think" (Ephesians 3:20, *NKJV*). God takes the "foolish things of the world to shame the wise; God chose the weak things of the world to shame the strong. He chose the lowly things of this world and the despised things—and the things that are not—to nullify the things that are, so that no one may boast before him. . . . Therefore, as it is written: 'Let him who boasts boast in the Lord' " (1 Corinthians 1:27-31).

Whatever your gift or talent or resources, there's a place of service for you in the King's court. Bring what you have to the feet of Jesus in undivided surrender . . . the Lord needs it! What do we learn from this man about a life of dedication to Jesus?

I. He First Gave Himself to Christ, Then His Resources.

A. He was a close friend to Jesus. He had put his faith in Christ. Because he had already given himself, he could easily give his possessions. He made himself at Christ's disposal in unreserved devotion. Until a man gives himself to God, he will hold tightly to everything he possesses. It's so easy to get wrapped up in ourselves and our possessions.

> Two hikers were walking through the woods when they suddenly confronted a giant bear. Immediately, one guy took off his boots, pulled out a pair of running shoes and began putting them on. "What are you doing?" asked the other man. "We can't outrun that bear, even with running shoes." "Who cares about the bear?" the first hiker replied. "All I have to worry about is outrunning you."

Illustration

B. What an amazing thing that the Lord would need anything from us. God is self-sufficient. His name, *Jehovah*, means "God is self-existent." He doesn't technically need anything. He is Jehovah-Jireh, the Lord our provider. Yet, He says to us, "I need you." The Lord needs your resources, talents, abilities and availability. Christ calls us into partnership with Himself in the building of His kingdom. God works in partnership with His people. The Holy Spirit is saying to you today, "The Lord needs it."

C. What talent, resource, financial strength, possession, or leadership gift is the Holy Spirit telling you to give to God in dedicated service? Once you give yourself totally to Christ, you will have no hesitancy giving up anything you possess for the kingdom of God.

II. His Only Motivation Was to Bring Glory to Jesus by Bringing Jesus to the People.

I find it interesting that this man remains unnamed. We all think recognition and showing appreciation to people is important.

A. *Motivation.* The Pharisees were motivated by name recognition (Matthew 23:5-12). Jesus said, "Do not let your left hand know what your right hand is doing" (6:3). President Ronald Reagan had a sign on his desk that read: "There's no limit to what a man can accomplish if he doesn't care who gets the credit."

B. *Honor.* The name we honor is the name of Jesus. We minister in His name, not our own. All of creation exists for Him (Philippians 2:9, 10; Colossians 1:16). The purpose of this man's gift was to provide the means by which Jesus could enter Jerusalem. He brought Jesus to the City. We do the same by the dedication of ourselves, our time, talent and treasure.

Illustration

Toscanini finished directing Beethoven's "Ninth Symphony" with brilliance. The crowd stood and cheered enthusiastically. Toscanini turned to the crowd and shouted over the applause, "Toscanini is nothing; Beethoven is everything!" We are nothing; Christ is everything!

III. He Gave the Best He Had, and His Gift Was Returned to Him Blessed by God.

A. The donkey had never been ridden. It represents giving God our best for sacred service. The man who gave the donkey counted it a privilege to be asked to help the cause of Christ. Giving is an honor and a privilege. The greatest return was that many others were blessed by his gift. Praise is more than a song; it is the continual giving of oneself for the honor of Jesus Christ. When he got the donkey back, he looked at it differently. That was his prized donkey because it had carried the Messiah. If I didn't know better, I would think he made that donkey a house pet. He was special.

B. We, too, can take ordinary talents and resources and take Jesus to the world. What we give always comes back blessed a hundred times over (Luke 6:38; Malachi 3:9, 10; 2 Corinthians 9:6, 7). The disciples thought they had given up a lot to follow Jesus until Jesus promised them a hundred times as much (Mark 10:28-30).

C. Personally I cannot speak of sacrifice in my own life. Every time I have given something to Him—time, talents and resources—He has used it, blessed it, and returned His blessings back a hundred times over. When Christ comes to where you live and says, "I need it," then give Him your all, and His blessings will overtake your life.

Christ Is Risen: So, What?

Easter Sermon

Text: Romans 6:1-4

Some years ago, construction workers in Jerusalem were digging near the site of Joseph of Arimathea's tomb. They found a skeleton that still had the nails that had been driven through the hands. Some skeptics thought the remains were the skeleton of Jesus. But the skeleton only proved that people were crucified 2,000 years ago. The remains were not those of Jesus. How can we be so sure? Because the triumphant church could have never been inspired to change the world by the skeleton of Jesus!

Skeletons and skeptics will always be around, but the passion of the early believers who carried the good news of Jesus to their world did not come from frightened followers who saw the skeleton of Jesus. To the contrary, they encountered the risen Christ! Today, over one-third of the world's population are devout followers of Jesus, and most other religions welcome Jesus. Furthermore, during the last five years of the 1990s, Christianity grew approximately 8 percent. An estimated 165,000 people come to know Christ every day. At this rate, nearly half the world's population will be Christian in only a few years (*Net Results* [Aug. 2000] 20).

The resurrection of Jesus is a historical fact. All early extra-Biblical sources agree that the tomb was empty. Rome admitted that the tomb was empty. The Jewish high court of the Sanhedrin admitted the tomb was empty. A cover-up story was issued. But nothing could change the fact that Jesus is alive!

- Abraham, the father of Judaism, lived 19 centuries before Christ—he has not risen.
- Buddha lived five centuries before Christ and died at age 80—he has not risen.
- Mohammed lived six centuries after Christ and died in A.D. 632. He's buried in Mecca— he has not risen.
- But when we visit the tomb of Jesus in Jerusalem, it is empty. The tomb still speaks: "Why do you look for the living among the dead? He is not here; he has risen!" (Luke 24:5, 6). So, what?

I. **The Resurrection Means a Vital Relationship With Jesus.**

   A. Easter is not the celebration of history, it is the celebration of experience. To simply believe intellectually that Jesus rose from the dead will not save us. Salvation comes when we personally meet the risen Lord and then believe in Him. His resurrection was marked by His personal appearances and presence with His people. They spent time with Him. For 40 days He met with them and taught them about the kingdom of God (Acts 1:3).

   B. He wanted them to know His presence. Then He returned to heaven and sent the Holy Spirit, who abides with us, giving us the experience of the presence of Christ. "I will not leave you as orphans; I will come to you" (John 14:18). Jesus promises us His living presence (Matthew 18:18-20; 28:20; Mark 16:20). The great invitation of the risen Christ is found in Revelation 3:20: "Behold, I stand at the door and knock" (*NKJV*).

***Barney and Jesus**. A little 4-year-old was seeing her pediatrician for a cold. He put the otoscope in her ear, looked around and said, "Do you think I find Big Bird in there?" She sat silent. Then he took his tongue depressor and inserted it in her mouth to look at her throat. "Do you think I find the Cookie Monster down there?" She just sat there silent. He then took his stethoscope and put it to her chest to listen to her heart. He said, "Do you think I find Barney in your heart?" She said, "Oh no, sir. Jesus is in my heart. Barney is on my underpants."

C. Paul asks, "Shall we go on sinning?" (Romans 6:1). *Sin,* here in this passage, refers to the sin nature within us all. Shall we go on habitually dominated by the old nature of sin? Absolutely not! Why? Because we have a relationship with the risen Christ. His will is our will. We want to live in such a way to allow nothing to break our relationship with Him.

D. Listen to Philippians 3:10, 11 and see the connection between "the power of his resurrection" and "I want to know Christ." Knowing the Person precedes knowing the power.

1. What would the cross be without the empty tomb? Just another death of a martyr. But the empty tomb completes His redemptive work on the cross.

2. Jesus did not die as a martyr. He died as a sacrifice for the sins of the world.

3. He rose again as Lord of all. So, I can sing, "I serve a risen Savior, He's in the world today, I know that He is living, whatever men may say. . . . You ask me how I know He lives? He lives within my heart."

II. The Resurrection Means Power for Living.

Paul makes two important statements about the power of the risen Christ in us who believe:

A. *We are dead to sin* (Romans 6:1, 6, 11, 12). Again, *sin* means the sin nature, the old self. Paul uses the imagery of baptism.

1. The early Christians, like the Jews, practiced baptism by immersion. The act of immersion reenacts Christ's death and resurrection, symbolized by the believer going down into the water (the grave) and then being raised out of the water (resurrection). We go from baptism, both spiritually and physically, to walk in the newness of life.

2. To be dead to sin means to be unresponsive to its temptations and influences. We are unmoved by sin's power. Sin has no control. You have a new nature, the nature of Christ. The new nature seeks to please God (8:5-11). You are a new creation (2 Corinthians 5:17).

B. *We are alive to God* (Romans 6:4, 11, 13). The new life is illustrated in the resurrection of Lazarus (John 11). Lazarus typifies every person who is dead in sin (Colossians 2:13). But Jesus walked up to the tomb and declared, "Lazarus, come forth!" (John 11:43, *NKJV*).

1. First, salvation is personal. He called him by name. Second, salvation comes through the Word of God. When we hear the good news of Jesus and believe His Word, we then come forth out of the tomb of sin and death to walk in newness of life (Romans 1:16; 10:17).

2. Then, Jesus said, "Take off the grave clothes and let him go" (John 11:44). That's a picture of spiritual growth. Once you are saved and raised from the death of sin, the Holy Spirit works in your life to take off the grave clothes, symbolic of the old life, and as you do, you are free!

3. The next time we see Lazarus in the Gospel of John, he is seated with Jesus at a banquet. You are now seated with Christ (Ephesians 2:4-6), and in eternity, He promises that we will sit with Him on His throne (Revelation 3:21).

C. *We are to consider what God says to be true* (Romans 6:11).

   1. *To consider* means to credit to one's account. The word is used 41 times in the New Testament, 19 of these in Romans. Believe what God says about you. You will live up to the view you have of yourself.

   2. If your self-concept is negative and defeated, that's how you will live. If your self-concept is rooted in Scripture and who you are in Christ, then you will live as sons and daughters of God.

III. The Resurrection Gives Meaning to the Moment (Romans 6:13).

A. To offer yourself to God means to place yourself at His disposal, to present yourself as a sacrifice (12:1).

   1. This is a conscious act of the will to live your life for the glory of the risen Christ. When Paul speaks of offering your body, he means the total self (1 Thessalonians 5:23).

   2. It takes all that I am and all that I have. To offer ourselves to God is a response of worship and praise for His salvation. We don't serve God out of fear but out of love. His will is our will. His purpose is our purpose. His command is our pleasure.

B. His resurrection gives meaning to my life.

   1. Today people are living at breakneck speed to enjoy the moment, but they live without spiritual purpose. Death is inevitable for us all.

   2. What, then, gives meaning to our existence? Why not follow the Epicureans and say, "Eat, drink, and be merry, for tomorrow we die"? Because we have the hope of eternal life. From the least to the greatest, we all have our appointment with death. But the resurrection of Christ assures us who trust Him that we shall share in His resurrection.

Illustration

Impact of the Christian life. The British explorer Henry Morgan Stanley visited missionary David Livingstone in Africa. After having spent considerable time with him, he said, "If I had been with him any longer, I would have been compelled to be a Christian, and he never spoke to me about it at all."

When Christ Returns

Text: 1 Thessalonians 4:14—5:11

Do you ever get the feeling that the world is spinning out of control? Paul Johnson, an English statesman, after surveying the chaotic conditions of the world, said, "There are times when I would welcome an invasion from Mars."

Well, an invasion will indeed come; not from Mars, but from heaven. The New Testament contains over 300 prophecies of the second of coming of Christ. In fact, one out of every 25 verses in the New Testament tells us that Jesus is coming again. A *U.S. News* poll found that nearly 60 percent of Americans think the world will end sometime in the future; almost a third of those think it will end within a few decades. More than 61 percent say they believe in the second coming of Christ. Nearly half believe the Antichrist will arise, and 44 percent believe a Battle of Armageddon will occur.

While the Bible does not give every detail about His return, and much of prophecy is shrouded in mystery, sealed up until the time of the end, one fact is clear: Jesus will return to earth again—visibly, literally and victoriously.

The worse the world becomes, the closer we draw to the return of Christ. The subject of the return of Christ is one of the most intriguing subjects in the Bible. Everyone is interested today in hearing about the return of Christ.

The Old Testament prophets foresaw it (Job 19:25, 26). Christ prophesied it (Matthew 24:27, 30-31). The angels announced it (Acts 1:9-11). The apostles anticipated it (1 Thessalonians 5:1-2; Jude 14). The Revelator envisioned it (1:7).

One of the greatest mysteries concerning the return of Christ is the rapture of the church. Christ's return will happen in two phases: First, He will receive His church in the Rapture; second, He will return at the end of the Great Tribulation with the saints and angels at Armageddon and establish the kingdom of God on earth. At the Rapture, He comes in the clouds of glory and we are caught up to meet Him. At the Advent, He comes at the end of the Great Tribulation to reign as King of kings.

I. The Rapture of the Church

A. The word *rapture* comes from the Latin *rapio*, which means "to catch away suddenly." While the word *rapture* does not actually appear in the Bible, the concept certainly appears clearly in 1 Thessalonians 4:16-18. "We . . . will be caught up" (v. 17). Let's break this passage down and look at the details.

B. Paul tells us "the Lord himself" (v. 16), meaning Jesus, won't send an angel or a messenger, but He is coming again personally. He will descend from heaven where He now reigns as our High Priest making intercession for us (Hebrews 7:25).

C. He will come with a shout of victory, letting us know that His second coming will not be quiet as was His first in Bethlehem. He is coming with the voice of the archangel, Michael, and a host of angels. The trumpet of God is going to sound. Then the dead in Christ will rise from their grave. Their spirits are with God in heaven now (see 2 Corinthians

5:8; Hebrews 12:23), but they will receive new resurrection bodies (see Philippians 3:21; 1 Corinthians 15:51-55).

D. Then "we who are still alive and are left will be caught up together with them in the clouds to meet the Lord in the air" (1 Thessalonians 4:17). Now that is about as clear as it can get that there will be a translation of God's people out of this world. It seems so far-fetched, and people ask, "Why will there be a Rapture?" I think I have a reasonable answer. The Rapture is not so that we can escape the Tribulation. Christians have suffered for 2,000 years the tribulation of persecution. I believe the Rapture is a final sign of God that the end is at hand and for this world to repent and turn to Him before the final Day of Judgment. God is patient, not wanting any to perish but for everyone to come to salvation (2 Peter 3:9).

E. The last thing Paul says is that we should "encourage each other with these words" about Christ's return (1 Thessalonians 4:18). While people have differing views on Bible prophecy and, especially, when the Rapture will take place, we don't need to argue, but to agree on the simple fact that He will return and leave the details to God!

II. The Revelation of Christ

A. The Bible describes the return of Christ at the end of the Great Tribulation, during which the Antichrist will arise, and the Battle of Armageddon will be fought. The Revelator describes His coming as Him being crowned King of kings and Lord of lords, with a sharp sword proceeding from His mouth to strike down the nations, and treading the winepress of the fury of the wrath of God Almighty (19:11-16).

B. His name is fully displayed for all to see. He comes as the absolute Lord and King, in the fullness of His power and authority.

Illustration

When Queen Elizabeth was crowned by the archbishop of Canterbury, he laid the crown on her head with the sure pronouncement, "I give thee, O Sovereign Lady, this crown to wear until He who reserves the right to wear it shall return."

   C. How different the second coming of Christ will be from His first coming into the world as our Savior.

     1. When He came the first time, He was meek and lowly of heart, but He will return as Judge of all the earth.

     2. When He came the first time, He was born in a manger; when He returns, He will be clothed with glory.

     3. When He came the first time, He was given a reed for a scepter; when He returns, He will rule the nations with a rod of iron.

     4. When He came the first time, He wore a crown of thorns; when He returns, He will be crowned with many crowns.

     5. When He came the first time, He was rejected, mocked and crucified; when He returns, every knee will bow before Him and every tongue confess that Jesus Christ is Lord to the glory of God the Father.

III. The Response of Faith.

   A. We need to pause and ask, What did the early church believe about the return of Christ? In response, while early Christians did not have an elaborately developed theology of the last days, they held firmly to the truth of the imminent return of Christ. That means they believed that Jesus could return at any time. For them, the Day of the Lord was always at hand. As John Walvoord points out: "The early church lived in constant expectation of the coming of the Lord for His church."

   B. Today, Christians need to live with the same level of expectant faith and joyful hope. As opposed to getting bogged down in theological debate, we need to be looking for "the blessed hope—the glorious appearing of our great God and Savior, Jesus Christ" (Titus 2:13).

C. Today, this means that no prophecies have to be fulfilled
    before Christ returns for His church. Since Christ's return
    could happen at any time, we are in a state of "ready-
    alert." Jesus said, "No one knows about that day or hour.
    . . . Therefore keep watch, because you do not know on
    what day your Lord will come. . . . So you also must be
    ready, because the Son of Man will come at an hour when
    you do not expect him" (Matthew 24:36, 42, 44).

D. The belief in the return of Christ should affect us in three
    ways:

    1. *Resilient faith.* Jesus asked, "When the Son of Man
        comes, will he find faith on the earth?" (Luke 18:8).
        Each person has to make their own decision about
        Christ and put their faith in Him. We also need to per-
        severe in our faith and not give up in tough times.

    2. *Radiant hope.* We are looking for "the blessed hope—
        the glorious appearing of our great God and Savior,
        Jesus Christ" (Titus 2:13). Without the promise of His
        return, there is no hope for the world.

        a. Bertrand Russell, the unbelieving British philoso-
            pher, wrote *Why I Am Not a Christian,* and said,
            "The best that we can hope for is unyielding
            despair."

        b. *Jesus described the world of the last days as a
            world of fear* (see Luke 21:26). Professor Harold
            Ure, a Nobel Prize winner, wrote in his book, *Man
            Afraid,* "I write this to frighten you. I am a fright-
            ened man. All the scientists I know are fright-
            ened—frightened for their lives and frightened for
            your life."

        c. *We live in a world of despair.* The threat of nuclear
            war hovers over our heads. Scientists tell us that if
            one hydrogen bomb encased in cobalt was detonat-
            ed over the North Pole, it would kill every living
            creature in the whole Northern Hemisphere of this

planet—3 billion people plus! Yet, in the midst of this world we have hope, and we can give hope (Titus 2:13).

3. *Responsive love.* His promise strengthens our love for Him, our Savior, and our love and concern for the world. "Grace to all who love our Lord Jesus Christ with an undying love" (Ephesians 6:24). We, then, should have a greater love and concern for the world that all might be saved. "For the love of Christ compels us," Paul said (2 Corinthians 5:14, *NKJV*).

4. Like Jesus, we need to be "moved with compassion" when we see the lost multitudes of our generation (Matthew 14:14).

Illustration

In 1996 George Tulloch led an exploration of the ruins of the sunken *Titanic*. He and his crew recovered numerous finds including eyeglasses, jewelry, fine china and various artifacts. In his search he realized that a large piece of the hull had broken off from the ship. He saw the opportunity to salvage a part of the famous ship. While the team attempted to raise the 22-ton piece of iron onto the boat, a storm blew in and kept them from gaining their treasure. Although the attempt failed, he resolved to return. But before he left, he descended two and one-half miles to the wreckage and, using the robotic arm of his submarine, attached a metal strip to the hull. On it, he had written: "I will come back, George Tulloch." Two years later, he returned and rescued the piece of iron.

Closing: Jesus left us with this promise: "I will come back. . . ." (John 14:1-3).

Walking in Truth

Text: 3 John 4

A leksandr Solzhenitsyn, in his Nobel Prize speech in Oslo, in 1974, said, "One word of truth outweighs the whole world." That's an amazing statement, since our planet has an area of about 196 million square miles and a mass of 6.57 sextillion tons (6.57 X 10^{21}). One of the greatest keys to living a healthy, happy and holy life is to live a life of truth.

But we live in an age that champions tolerance over truth. People are hesitant to stand for truth for fear of being labeled extremist, judgmental or unkind. Sure, we are to be tolerant of others' viewpoints and opinions. But tolerance is not a moral principle—truth is. Our age likes to talk about values instead of morals. You see, values are relative. Truth is absolute. Groups organize themselves around values every day. Even street gangs have values, but they don't live moral truth. They lie for each other, protect each other, and stick together regardless. But truth condemns their behavior as criminal.

Corporations have values such as teamwork, productivity, leadership, excellence and efficiency, but without moral truth such as love for neighbor, integrity, sacrifice and benevolence, the corporation's values are worthless.

America is guided by the Constitution, which serves as a document of principles to which every leader and citizen is to submit himself. No person is above the law. The nation is based on principles—principles that are absolute, as seen in the Declaration of Independence: "We hold these truths to be self-evident. . . ." Notice the emphasis on truth.

The apostle Paul said, "We cannot do anything against the truth, but only for the truth" (2 Corinthians 13:8). Isaiah 59:14, 15 says, "Truth has stumbled in the streets, honesty cannot enter. Truth is nowhere to be found." Jeremiah 7:28 says, "Truth has perished; it has vanished from their lips." Daniel 8:12 says, "Truth was thrown to the ground." Proverbs 23:23 says, "Buy the truth and do not sell it." Romans 1:25 says, "They exchanged the truth of God for a lie." Paul says that in the last days people will be "always learning but never able to acknowledge the truth" (2 Timothy 3:7). As believers, we are called to a lifestyle of truth (John 4:24; Ephesians 4:15; 6:14; 1 Timothy 3:15). Jesus said, "You will know the truth, and the truth will set you free" (John 8:32). Pilate asked Christ, "What is truth?" (18:38). The answer comes: "I am the way and the truth and the life" (14:6).

Illustration

Fly for Half Price. There are those who live by the ethic that everything is permissible as long as you don't get caught. I heard about a mother who was taking her little boy to the airport to buy an airline ticket. He was 6 years old and quite small for his age. She knew that children 4 years old and younger got to fly for half price. So she told her son to say he was 4 if asked by the agent. Walking up to the ticket counter, she sat her little boy on the counter and ordered her tickets. The agent thought he looked a little big for 4 years old, so she asked the little fellow, "So, how old are you?" "I'm 4," he answered. The agent looked closely at him and said, "Do you know what happens to little boys who lie about their age?" He said, "Yes ma'am, they get to fly for half price."

I.   Be Truthful With God.

Proverbs 12:22 says, "The Lord detests lying lips, but he

delights in men who are truthful." Psalm 51:6 says, "You desire truth in the inner parts." There are three barriers to honesty with God:

A. *Rationalization.* Rationalization says, "My sins are not as bad as those others are committing." When we rationalize our sins, we make the mistake of comparing our sins with other sinners instead of comparing our sin with the holiness of Christ. Or, we may conclude that because everybody else is doing it, then it's OK. But running with the pack is risky business.

B. *Justification.* We tell ourselves that we are exceptions to the rules. In his classic novel, *War and Peace,* Leo Tolstoy's primary character, Pierre, is convicted of his sins, but he makes the mistake of praying, "O Lord, I have sinned, but I have several excellent excuses."

C. *Projection.* We quickly discern and judge the sins of others so that we don't have to deal with our own sins. Like a camera, we project our sins onto others. After all, it's easier to see their sins than it is to see our own. And it is certainly easier to judge others than it is to judge ourselves. But then we hear the apostle tell us, "Examine yourselves . . . test yourselves" (2 Corinthians 13:5). As Plato said, "The unexamined life is not worth living."

II. Be Truthful With Others.

The Bible says to speak the truth in love and that each of us is to "put off falsehood and speak truthfully to his neighbor" (Ephesians 4:15, 25).

A. *In regard to relationships.* Lying and deceit causes people not to trust us. Close relationships are built on trust. As a parent, I always told my kids to be honest. No matter what they did, if they were honest, it would be better for them, and we could work things out. But when we deceive, we create greater problems.

B. *In regard to sins.* Not only do we need to confess to God, we need to confess our sins to each other. In fact, this is a key to healing. The Bible says, "Confess your sins to each other and pray for each other so that you may be healed. The prayer of a righteous man is powerful and effective" (James 5:16). Share with someone you can trust.

III. Be Truthful With Yourself.

A. Shakespeare said, "To thine own self be true." We also need to be honest in our self-expression. You may remember the popular book written in the '70s by Eric Berne titled, *Games People Play.* It explained the process of transactional analysis in human relationships. The book helped identify the "defense mechanisms" we use, which are ways we hide from each other, and the games we play in order to get people to love and accept us.

B. Instead of expressing ourselves, we play games trying to figure out what people want from us so that they will love us. Unfortunately, the game never works. You only end up losing touch with who you are and feeling rejected and unloved by all the people you're trying to please.

C. I read that when we are in our 20s, we worry about what people think of us. In our 40s we don't care what they think, and in our 60s we realize they haven't been thinking about us at all!

D. There is no one in the world just like you. You are unique, and you bring something unique to this world that your family, friends and associates need from you. The church needs your gifts and service so that it can be all that it is designed to be.

Closing: The church is only whole when all the parts of the body are fully functioning (see 1 Corinthians 12:27). So let your light shine—the unique, individual light of your personality. Take off the mask. Stop hiding and playing games. To your own self be true!

"Who Is My Neighbor?"

Text: Luke 10:25-37

O ne of the best ways to learn is to ask questions. Children are fond of asking a lot of questions. A little boy tugged on his father's sleeve one evening, just as his father settled in his recliner to read the newspaper. "Daddy, how hot is the sun?" His father, not wanting to be bothered, responded, "Son, I don't know." Tugging again on his sleeve, the boy inquired enthusiastically, "Daddy, how far away is the moon?" "Son, I don't know." "Daddy, why is a horse bigger than a dog?" "Son, I really don't know," the father responded rather irritated. Pulling his father's sleeve again, he asked softly, "Daddy, do you mind me asking you all these questions?" Looking up from his paper, the father says, "Heavens no, Son. If you don't ask questions, how are you ever going to learn anything?"

People were fond of asking Jesus questions, especially religious leaders. One day a teacher of the Law, that is, the Scripture, asked Jesus two very important questions. The first was the right question, but he had the wrong answer. The second was the wrong question, and Jesus gave him the right answer.

I. The Right Question and the Wrong Answer

A. *The question*: "What must I do to inherit eternal life?" (v. 25). This question concerns us all, regardless of who we are. He was a man who spent his life studying the Scriptures. This was one of the most profound spiritual questions the rabbis considered. He was asking how to have the life of the kingdom of God, just as Nicodemus did (see John 3:1-4). Until this question is satisfactorily answered, no one has peace of mind.

B. *The motive*: "To test Jesus" (Luke 10:25). The man was not entirely pure in his motives. He wanted to test Jesus, maybe to cause Him to incriminate Himself in something He said, or perhaps to see what kind of teacher He was. So this parable was told in a highly charged religious environment.

C. *The answer*: Jesus asked him a question to direct him to the right answer: "What does the Scripture say?" (See v. 26). Christ did not ask him, "What do you think?" Or, "What do the rabbis teach?" Or, "What do the public opinion polls say?" He turns to the Scripture—the same place we need to turn to when asking the great questions of life. The answer is to love God and love your neighbor. Jesus said, "Do this and you will live" (v. 28). Now, the teacher of the Law wore a phylactery containing the very answer he sought (Deuteronomy 6:5-9). People today have heard the gospel, they wear it as if it were in their minds every day, but they fail to believe it.

D. *The problem and the solution*: "But he wanted to justify himself, so he asked Jesus, 'And who is my neighbor?'" (Luke 10:29). Here was a man who could look at the Law of God and fail to see his own sinfulness. He wanted to justify himself, to make himself righteous. The Law reveals our unrighteousness and leads us to the grace of God. Archbishop Fulton Sheen spoke at the National Prayer Breakfast during Jimmy Carter's presidency. He began his

address, "Mr. President, Mrs. Carter and fellow sinners . . ."
Once he had everyone's attention, he went on to talk about
sin and God's cure. No one has kept all the Law (Romans
3:23; James 2:10). The Law reveals our sin and leads us to
Jesus, who alone can save us from the penalty and power
of sin (Galatians 3:24). The solution for our failure of the
Law is to be justified by faith alone (Romans 5:1; 8:1;
Ephesians 2:8, 9).

II. The Wrong Question and the Right Answer

A. *The wrong question*: "Who is my neighbor?" (Luke
10:29). The question implies that love can be selective in
the object it chooses to love. So, Jesus changed the question to be, What does it mean to be a neighbor? The question is not, Whom should we love? but rather, How should
we love?

B. *The right answer*: Jesus taught that the royal law of love
is the foundation of all Scripture (Matthew 22:37-40; John
13:34, 35; James 2:8). He tells the story of the Good
Samaritan to show us the way to live abundantly. To most
Pharisees, no Samaritan was good. Jesus could have told
the story as a Samaritan who had been robbed and a Jew
who rescued him. But Jesus tells the story in such a way
to get the Pharisee to confront himself and look at the real
attitudes of his heart.

C. *The victim*. The old Jericho road was a treacherous road,
winding down through the mountains with steep cliffs and
narrow passageways. It stretched 15 miles from Jerusalem
to Jericho. It was known for being a hideout for robbers
who would lie in wait for innocent victims.

D. *The priest and the Levite.*

1. Jericho was the town of the priests and Levites who
served at the Temple in Jerusalem. They were divided
into groups who rotated their time of service throughout the year. The most important role of the priest was

to offer the sacrifices. The Levites served to maintain the Temple services and order and to assist the priests.

2. They were both on their way home from Jerusalem. They were going down as opposed to going up to Jerusalem. Jerusalem is always mentioned as being "up" in Scripture since it is the highest and most sacred place. They were also traveling alone. The priests and Levites traveled in groups when they went up to Jerusalem to perform their service.

3. Why did they not help the man? Many reasons could be given:

    a. Some have suggested that they thought he was dead. If they had touched him, they would have been ceremonially unclean and, thus, unable to serve at the Temple for a period of time. But they weren't going to the Temple, they were going home.

    b. They may have thought it was a trap, or a setup to rob them.

    c. Perhaps they thought he had gotten what he deserved.

4. Whatever the motive, they didn't care about the man. That's why they passed by. They were busy with their own schedules, focused on themselves and too self-absorbed to get involved. They were religion at its worst. They kept their traditions and laws they wrote, but failed the greatest test of all: Do you love your neighbor as you love yourself? This is the Law we will all be judged by (James 2:12, 13).

E. *The Good Samaritan.* The fact that Jesus called the Samaritan "good" is interesting. Most Pharisees would have considered no Samaritan to be good. Who were the Samaritans? After the Assyrian invasion of Israel (722 B.C.), Jews intermarried with other nationalities that were brought to live in Israel by the Assyrians. So, they were no longer a pure Jewish lineage in Christ's time. They were rejected by Orthodox Jews. A great racial divide existed between the two groups. The Samaritans lived in the eastern portion of Israel with their own temple on Mount Gerizim, since they were not permitted in the Jerusalem Temple. Jewish rabbis avoided entering Samaritan cities. But Jesus often went to Samaria to preach and minister. What does the Good Samaritan teach us about love?

1. *Love transcends barriers*. He came to where the man was. What a portrait of grace. God came to us in Jesus (Romans 5:8). He didn't mind that the wounded man was a Jew. He transcended the barriers of race, ethnicity and creed (Galatians 3:26). Love does not discriminate on the basis of race, belief, lifestyle, religion or social status. Love, like God, is no respecter of persons. Love does not consider the condition of the people it loves.

2. *Love sees clearly*. He saw him and took pity on him. I am struck by the words "he saw him" (Luke 10:33). The priest and the Levite saw him too, but not in the same way. We see people every day in need of God, but do we really see them? The priest and the Levite saw the man with a look of curiosity, or judgment, or indifference, or even fear. Let's give them the benefit of the doubt and say they were too afraid of getting involved. But the Samaritan saw him with the eyes of God. People look different when we see them like God sees them.

3. *Love feels deeply*. The word for *pity* means "compassion." Compassion is the emotional side of love (Matthew 9:36; 14:14; 15:32; 18:27). Jesus also used this word to describe the rich man who forgave the dishonest servant (18:23-27) and the father who forgave

his Prodigal Son (Luke 15:11-32). Love considers how it has been loved and, in turn, loves much.

4. *Love sacrifices greatly*. There is a sacrifice to true love. He "bandaged his wounds" (10:34). Maybe he had to tear off strips of his own clothes to make the bandages. What a portrait of what it means to be healers! He bandaged the wounds and poured on the oil and wine (Holy Spirit). We have something wonderful to give the world in the good news of Christ (Luke 4:18, 19).

5. *Love remembers faithfully*. He took him to an inn. The "next day" he returned to check on the man and paid the hotel fee (10:35). He promised to return. Have you ever been forgotten by someone when you needed him or her? God remembers us in our distress.

Closing: Now back to the original question: "What must I do?" Jesus answers, "Go and do likewise" (v. 37). God does not bestow the life of the Kingdom on those who reject the command to love. Such rejection shows that they do not realize how much they need the love of God themselves.

How to Get a Promotion

Text: Luke 14:15-24

Many years ago a man came to America from Europe, and after being processed at Ellis Island, went into a cafeteria in New York City to get something to eat. He sat down at an empty table and waited for someone to take his order. Of course, nobody did. Finally, a man with a tray of delicious food sat down near him and told him how things worked. "Start at the end," he said, "and pick out what you want. At the other end they'll tell you how much you owe." "I soon learned that's how everything works in America," he said. "Life is a cafeteria. You can get anything you want as long as you're willing to pay the price. You can even get success. But you'll never get it if you wait for someone to bring it to you. You have to get up and get it yourself."

We all want to get ahead in life, but sometimes we're not sure how. We want to better our lifestyles and get promoted. But how do you get a promotion? Promotion comes from God (Psalm 75:6, 7). Jesus told us how to get a promotion in His parable of the wedding feast (Luke 14:15-24).

Jesus was attending a banquet at the home of a prominent Pharisee. The words of Jesus ring true today: "The exalted will be humbled, the humble will be exalted" (see v. 11). When God places His hand on your life and endows you with His favor, there is absolutely nothing or no one who can keep you from reaching the fullness of your potential for the glory of God. For if God be for you, who can be against you? (Romans 8:31).

I.   The Exalted Will Be Humbled.

A.   Jesus warns us against the pitfall of pride. An officer aboard the *Titanic* boasted, "God himself could not sink this ship." The way of the world is to promote yourself. The way of the Kingdom is to humble yourself and allow God to promote you. Pride will bring every person, every family, every organization, every nation down from its lofty place. Proverbs 29:23 states, "A man's pride brings him low, but a man of lowly spirit gains honor."

B.   *What is pride?* *Pride,* in its evil sense, means "an undue sense of one's superiority; inordinate self-esteem; arrogance; conceit." Such pride is sin. "Haughty eyes and a proud heart, the lamp of the wicked, are sin!" (21:4). Now there is an honorable sense of pride and self-esteem (2 Corinthians 7:4).

C.   *What does pride produce?*

1.   Dominance of the weak—"In his arrogance the wicked man hunts down the weak, who are caught in the schemes he devises" (Psalm 10:2).

2.   Violence—"Therefore pride is their necklace; they clothe themselves with violence" (73:6).

3.   Disgrace—"When pride comes, then comes disgrace, but with humility comes wisdom" (Proverbs 11:2).

4.   Destruction—"Pride goes before destruction, a haughty spirit before a fall" (16:18). How many lives, marriages, homes, businesses and ministries have been destroyed by pride?

5. Judgment—"The Lord Almighty has a day in store for all the proud and lofty, for all that is exalted (and they will be humbled)" (Isaiah 2:12).

6. Alienation from God (1 John 2:15-17).

The story of King Nebuchadnezzar is a classic example of both the downfall of pride and the exaltation God gives when we honor Him (see Daniel 4:28-37). He boasted, "Is not this the great Babylon I have built?" (v. 30). God disciplined him for his pride. He was insane for seven years until he, in his own words, "raised my eyes toward heaven, and my sanity was restored" (v. 34). After his restoration he acknowledged that God is sovereign over the kingdom of men. He gave praise to God, and God blessed him.

Illustration

II. The Humble Person Will Be Exalted.

A. *What is humility?* Andrew Murray wrote: "Humility is perfect quietness of heart. It is to expect nothing, to wonder at nothing that is done to me, to feel nothing done against me. It is to be at rest when nobody praises me, and when I am blamed or despised. It is to have a blessed home in the Lord, where I can go in and shut the door, and kneel to my Father in secret, and am at peace as in a deep sea of calmness, when all around and above is trouble."

B. *The blessing of humility.* Martin Luther said, "Nothing puts a person farther out of the devil's reach as does humility." We are told of the power of humility in Scripture: "Humility comes before honor" (Proverbs 15:33)."Humble yourselves before the Lord, and he will lift you up" (James 4:10). "God opposes the proud but gives grace to the humble" (1 Peter 5:5).

C. *How is it cultivated?* There are two ways: externally and internally.

1. *God cultivates humility in us externally by the experiences of life.*

a. *Through the discipline of hard work.* The work ethic is one of the most important lessons for character development. When we work for what we have, we live with a sense of appreciation and gratitude to God.

b. *God uses the difficulties of life.* Brokenness comes from the tough experiences of life when we come to the end of ourselves and rely on God. You really have to come to the end of yourself and stop believing your own press if you want God to promote you. When we're young, it's easy to be prideful, overidealistic and opinionated, having all the answers. But as we deal with life on its own terms and go through disappointments and failures and pains, we tend to rely more and more on God. That's why the apostle Peter exhorted young people, "Clothe yourselves with humility" (1 Peter 5:5).

Illustration

Booker T. Washington was a great man of humility. In his youth he walked hundreds of miles to one of the few universities that accepted black students. When he arrived he was told that the classes were full. He was offered a job making beds and sweeping floors. He made the beds and swept the floors so well that it wasn't long before his supervisors noticed his diligence and accepted him into the university. He went on to become one of the great scholars of his day. The point is—only the little man refuses the little task.

2. *God cultivates humility in us internally by the work of the Holy Spirit.* He conforms us into the image of Christ. He continually lifts up before us the model of Christ, who says, "Follow Me." Only the Holy Spirit working in us can bring forth the fruit of humility (Matthew 11:28-30; Philippians 2:5, 8).

D. *What does it mean to be exalted?* The Greek word *hupsoo* means "to lift up, to raise high to a place of honor."

1. *Exaltation does not always mean the same thing it does in worldly terms. Exaltation* does not mean fame,

fortune, power or pleasure. It does mean "the fullness of the blessing of God." God will exalt you to the place where He desires for you to serve. The exalted place is often the place of servitude to others. Who's the greatest? Jesus said, "I am among you as one who serves" (see Luke 22:24-27). One of the tests of humility is your ability to rejoice when others receive promotion ahead of you. Pride is envious and jealous.

2. *Exaltation takes place in God's time.* God exalts His people *in due time.* Humility, then, demands full submission to the will of God (1 Peter 5:6).

3. *Exaltation is a sure promise from the Lord.* The humble *will be* exalted. If you honor God, you will experience Psalm 1:1-3. The greatest exaltation will not even come in this life, but when we face the Lord of eternity and heaven evaluates the success of our lives.

The Temptation

Text: Matthew 4:1-11

He was known as the silver-tongued orator of Rome. He was a great statesman and a courageous soldier. As far as personal qualities are concerned, he could have been a world ruler. His name was Mark Anthony. In spite of his notable qualities, however, he possessed a great moral flaw in his character. So much so that on one occasion his personal tutor shouted in his face, "O Marcus, O colossal child! Able to conquer the world but unable to resist a temptation."

How well do we fare when temptation comes our way? The temptation experience of Christ is recorded in Scripture for us that we may learn how to overcome temptation. The only way the disciples knew of Christ's temptation was that He told them. He shared His experience to help them when they faced temptation.

The time of His temptation is significant. He had just been baptized by John. It was a confirming moment in His life. The Spirit anointed Him for His work, and the Father spoke: "This is My beloved Son" (3:17, *NKJV*). John announced to the crowds, "Behold! The Lamb of God who takes away the sin of the world!" (John 1:29, *NKJV*). Immediately after this incredible experience,

Jesus was led by the Spirit into the desert to be tempted by the devil. He went into the desert to be alone with God—to sort out His calling—to decide how He was to fulfill the calling of Messiah.

He fasted and prayed for 40 days in the desert. The desert is a place of solitude, preparation and testing in Scripture. God tested and prepared Moses in the desert for 40 years. The number 40 is used in Scripture to denote a time of testing and communion with God. Moses was with God on Mount Sinai for 40 days (Exodus 24:18). Elijah was in the wilderness for 40 days when God spoke to him in the "still small voice" (1 Kings 19:8, 12). Mark adds that Jesus was with the wild animals, perhaps adding to the portrait of Christ's solitude (1:13).

The devil tempted Him in an effort to defeat Him in carrying out the will of God. This is the bottom line of all temptation. But Jesus overcame him! The temptations Christ faced are the ones we, too, must face and defeat if we are to do the will of God. What do we learn?

I.   Temptation Is No Respecter of Persons.

　　A.   Everyone gets tempted. Even Christ was tempted in every way as we are, yet without sin (Hebrews 4:15). His temptation was real. It was not playacting. He faced greater temptations than we do. Satan doesn't have to use his full force against us, but he did against Christ. Hebrews 2:18 says that because Christ suffered when He was tempted, He is able to help those who are being tempted. No one is beyond the reach of temptation.

　　B.   No one grows so much spiritually that he or she is beyond getting tempted. Now, the people who tell you they never get tempted, well, you know their area of weakness—lying.

Illustration　　Three preachers were having breakfast one day. They were talking about spiritual accountability and decided they should be accountable to each other. So they decided that they would share their sins since the Bible says to confess your sins to each other. The first said, "I have always had a problem with lying. In fact, I often lie to the deacons." The second said, "I have a problem with stealing. Sometimes I take a little extra from the offering when I'm in a bind." The third minister said, "I have a problem with the sin of gossip, and I can't wait to get out of here and tell what I've heard today!"

II. Temptation Comes in Two Forms.

A. *Temptation to sin. To tempt* means "to allure, to entice and to seduce" (see James 1:13-15). The Lord's Prayer, "Lead us not into temptation" (Matthew 6:13), means "Don't allow us to be misled by the tempter." Just as the tempter came to Adam and Eve in the Garden, he comes to us. The word *temptation* comes from fishing. It means "to allure" the way that bait is used to allure a fish off course. It sees the bait and snatches it, thinking it has just swallowed a delicious meal, only to find itself ensnared. Temptation catches you totally off guard and ensnares you while you think you are having such a good time.

B. *Temptation as testing* (James 1:12). Temptation also takes the form of testing. We cannot overlook the statement that Jesus was "led by the Spirit . . . to be tempted," or to be tested. Now we know that God does not tempt one to sin. The desert was a time of divine preparation for ministry. During that time, the devil came to tempt Him. God *tests* us, while the devil *tempts.* God tests us in order to develop us. We are tested by life's adversities and disappointments. God tested Abraham (Genesis 22:1). God does not test us to defeat us, but to develop us; not to make us bitter, but to make us better.

III. Temptations Are Recycled.

A. Even though Jesus defeated him, Satan later returned (Luke 4:13). He returned at a more opportune time. Don't get discouraged when at a later time, you face the enemy you have just defeated. Being tempted is not a sign of spiritual weakness. If fact, it is an evidence of true conversion. Only those who desire to follow Christ are hit with temptations.

B. Some Christians worry about their spiritual condition because they are still subject to temptation. They mistakenly think that they can and will arrive at a place where they are no longer tempted.

C. Christ never reached that place. It is beyond reach in this life. As long as we are in this world, we will face temptation and testing. Satan came to Christ later when Peter tried to prevent Him from going to the Cross (Matthew 16:23). His greatest battle was in Gethsemane, which He won by praying, "Not my will, but yours be done" (Luke 22:42).

IV. Temptation Often Follows on the Heels of a Great Spiritual Experience.

A. Great spiritual experiences do not make us less susceptible to temptation; they make us more invincible when temptation comes. The writers of the Gospels stress the immediacy of the Temptation after Jesus' baptism.

B. We need to be on guard after a great spiritual experience. Elijah fell prey to fear, depression and self-doubt immediately after defeating the prophets of Baal and calling fire from heaven. He went from the pinnacle of victory to the valley of defeat.

C. Jesus speaks of those who start their walk with Him with great enthusiasm only to find the seed of the Word stolen from their heart by the devil or from being defeated by temptation because they have no spiritual roots (Mark 4:17). God does not want us to live manic-depressive or bipolar spiritual lives with ups and downs. The safest route is the way of stability and consistency. So, be on guard after a great spiritual experience. Remember, it's when you're on the mountain peak that the devil comes. If you are away from God, he doesn't need to tempt you; you've already yielded to it.

D. The more opportune time of the devil is when we are riding high, feeling like we're invincible: "If you think you are standing firm, be careful that you don't fall" (1 Corinthians 10:12).

Several years ago a minister I know was in a restaurant having breakfast with his wife. He noticed a man come in the restaurant who was a minister on staff at another church. They struck up a conversation, and my friend asked how he was doing and how the church was doing. "I'm no longer in the ministry," he replied. Shocked, my friend said, "What happened?" He said, "I got caught off guard and fell into sin." Then he said, "Be careful. Be on your guard."

V. Temptation Can Be Conquered.

A. Christ overcame, and He will enable us to overcome if we follow His example. The same Christ who defeated the devil in the wilderness will defeat him in your life. Jesus replied, "It is written" (Matthew 4:4). His mind was filled with the Scripture.

B. You have to see yourself as a victor if you are to be victorious. Many battles are lost before they are ever fought because we expect to be defeated. We suffer from self-doubt instead of trusting the power of the risen Lord.

C. Repeat with me: *Greater is He that is in me than he that is the world!* (John 4:4). Because Christ lives in us, He imparts to us His victory and power. He lives out His victory in us. It is a mystery, but a great reality—Christ lives in me (Galatians 2:20).

D. Victory is a process. The more we face the repetitive temptations. The stronger we grow. We all yield to temptation. We all fall down. Get back up (Micah 7:8). When we do, let us go to God and confess our sins. Then get back up and "press toward the mark for the prize of the high calling of God" (Philippians 3:14, KJV).

Closing: Here's God's promise to us in times of temptation: "No temptation has seized you except what is common to man. And God is faithful; he will not let you be tempted beyond what you can bear. But when you are tempted, he will also provide a way out so that you can stand up under it" (1 Corinthians 10:13).

The Blood Still Speaks

Text: Hebrews 12:22-24

Today we are confronted with a question of supreme impor-tance: *Why did Christ come into the world?* We tend to con-fuse what Christ did with why He came. Indeed, He preached the kingdom of God. He healed the sick and performed signs and won-ders to confirm the Kingdom message. He showed us the way of love. But He came for only one reason: to save us from our sins (Matthew 1:21; 1 Timothy 1:15).

This is why the Bible places such emphasis on the blood of Christ shed on the cross. It is by His blood that we are saved. Leviticus 17:11 says, "The life of a creature is in the blood, and I have given it to you to make atonement for yourselves on the altar; it is the blood that makes atonement for one's life." The blood is mentioned over 700 times in Scripture. The word *blood* is a syn-onym for *life*. So when the Bible speaks of the blood of Christ, it means His sacrificial life given for our sins on the cross.

His blood is a covenant blood (Matthew 26:28), a justifying blood (Romans 5:9), a forgiving blood (Ephesians 1:7), a reconcil-ing blood (2:13), a cleansing blood (1 John 1:7), a sanctifying blood (Hebrews 13:12), and a redeeming blood (Revelation 1:5).

So we join the host of heaven and sing Revelation 5:9, 10. The cross is not an emblem, but a sign of victory. On the cross Christ redeemed us from our sins. He lifted his voice in victory, "It is finished" (John 19:30). This was the cry of a Roman general, which he would declare to his troops when a battle had turned in their favor. Sin is finished! Death is finished! The law is finished! Redemption is finished! The plan of salvation is finished!

There is a communication breakdown when preaching on the blood to the 21st-century mind. We are so far removed from the sacrificial system that we struggle to connect with the imagery.

I.   The Blood Speaks.

A. The writer of Hebrews gives a contrast between the blood of Abel and the blood Christ. Cain murdered his brother, Abel. God confronted Cain: "Listen! Your brother's blood cries out to me from the ground" (Genesis 4:10). The blood of Abel cries for justice. It is the blood of the martyrs (Revelation 6:9, 10). But Jesus speaks a better word. His blood cries out to God for mercy.

B. On the Day of Atonement, the high priest entered the Holy of Holies in the Temple with the blood of the sacrifice, which had been offered on the brazen altar in the courtyard. He wore only the linen ephod. He carried the blood in a censer. He passed through the Holy Place, behind the veil, into the Holy of Holies. He then sprinkled the blood seven times, representing completion or perfection, on the cover of the ark of the covenant between the gold cherubim. He made *atonement*, which means "to cover," for the sins of the people. God's glory would appear in the Holy of Holies when the blood was sprinkled. The blood covered the voice of the Law within the ark and spoke a word of mercy and intercession. *The blood says, "The penalty has been paid, the demands of justice have been met, and so, the guilty are pardoned from all guilt."*

C. When He was resurrected He went into heaven and presented His own blood before the altar of God and made atonement for our sins. Today we can approach God freely and confidently because the Blood speaks on our behalf (1 John 2:1, 2).

II. The Blood Is Sufficient.

A. The blood of the Old Testament sacrifices could not atone for sins (Hebrews 9:22; 10:4). They were only symbols of the blood of Christ. His blood is precious (1 Peter 1:19). The Virgin Birth confirms the sinlessness of Christ. This is the crucial truth. Only a sinless Savior could atone for our sins. The bloodline of Adam versus Christ is emphasized by Paul (Romans 5:12-21).

B. The blood of a child is different from the blood of the mother. The blood of a child is only produced when the sperm and ovum (egg) unite and the fetus begins to develop. So, the child has its own blood separate from the mother. At no point during pregnancy does the blood of the mother come into contact with the fetus. The placenta forms a link between the mother and the child. It allows all soluble elements such as proteins, fats, carbohydrates, minerals and even antibodies to pass freely from mother to child, and also for waste products from the child to be passed back to the mother. Yet, no actual interchange of blood occurs. All the blood of the child's is produced within the fetus itself (M.R. DeHaan, *The Chemistry of the Blood*).

C. The blood of animals can never take away sins. The animals only pointed to the blood of Christ. Christ has no need of the offerings of the Old Testament order. He has no need of the burnt, the grain, the fellowship, the sin or the guilt offering. He is the offering of God for the sins of the world. After His resurrection He entered heaven itself with His own blood and presented it before the altar of God. And 2,000 years later the Blood still speaks on our behalf and says, "Come boldly to the throne of grace, that [you] may obtain mercy and find grace to help in time of need" (Hebrews 4:16, *NKJV*).

III. The Blood Must Be Sprinkled.

A. Note that the writer of Hebrews says we have come "to Jesus the mediator of a new covenant, and to the sprinkled blood (12:24). The sprinkling of the atoning blood means to apply its power to one's life. There were five predominant uses of the sprinkled blood in the Old Testament.

1. The Passover (Exodus 12:22)
2. When the covenant of the Law was ratified, Moses sprinkled the blood on the people (24:7, 8).
3. The Tabernacle and its furniture were consecrated by blood (Hebrews 9:21).
4. The consecration of Aaron and his sons as priests (Exodus 29:20)
5. The Day of Atonement on the mercy seat (Leviticus 16:15, 16)

B. The blood on the altar will not save us. Only when the Blood is applied are we saved. The cleansing power of the blood of Christ is applied by faith to our hearts (Hebrews 9:11-14). How can the Blood be applied? Through faith in Christ (Romans 10:9, 10). When you truly believe that Christ is the Son of God and you confess your sins to Him, the power of His blood cleanses your sins, and you are saved from sin and for a life of worship to God. The Blood can be sprinkled on your heart, your mind, your home, your children, your problems. It is a blood of cleansing, consecration and deliverance. No person could sprinkle the blood on himself. A priest had to sprinkle the blood. Jesus is the Priest of the world. Come to Him and pray, "Lord Jesus, sprinkle my heart with Your blood."

Closing: It is more than a religious cliché. It is a powerful truth: "There is power, power, wonder-working power in the precious blood of the Lamb." *The blood still speaks!*